Library of Congress Control Number: 2008929190
International Standard Book Number: 978-1-59979-399-3

08 09 10 11 12 — 987654321
Printed in the United States of America

I have known evangelist Asfaw Berhane for almost two years now. We work together; he's always been a great example of a man of God, a man of integrity. We often talk about the dreams and visions that God gives him. Brother Asfaw is always ready to pray for you if you need it and to encourage you. This book is such a blessing to me.

Heaven Is Empty, Hell Is Full will give you chills, chills of excitement over heaven and the presence of God and chills of dread regarding hell; the sight of the people there bobbing up and down in the flames, screaming, yelling, and praying. Their cries will not be heard; their prayers will not be answered. But we do hear them in the here and now, and we preach on street corners, "Fill up heaven and quit filling up hell." Jesus told Evangelist Asfaw to tell the world and all Christians alike, "Fill up heaven, not hell." Listen to the Word of God: "Save others by snatching them out of the fire [of hell]" (Jude 23, NRSV). It is the duty and command of our God to do so.

—Pastor Jerome and Josie Weymouth
Associate pastors,
South El Monte Praise Chapel

HEAVEN IS EMPTY, HELL IS FULL by Asfaw D. Berhane
Published by Creation House
A Strang Company
600 Rinehart Road
Lake Mary, Florida 32746
www.creationhouse.com

Unless otherwise noted, all Scripture quotations are from the New King James Version of the Bible. Copyright © 1979, 1980, 1982 by Thomas Nelson, Inc., publishers. Used by permission.

Scripture quotations marked KJV are from the King James Version of the Bible.

Scripture quotations marked NIV are from the Holy Bible, New International Version. Copyright © 1973, 1078, 1984, International Bible Society. Used by permission.

Scripture quotations marked NRSV are from the New Revised Standard Version of the Bible. Copyright © 1989 by the Division of Christian Education of the National Council of the Churches of Christ in the USA. Used by permission.

Design Director: Bill Johnson
Cover design by Karen Grindley

HEAVEN
IS EMPTY
H LL
IS FULL

ASFAW D. BERHANE

CREATION
HOUSE

DEDICATION

*I want to dedicate this book to the
Father, the Son, and the Holy Spirit
and to all God's generals of our time for
their faithfulness, their loyalty, their
trustworthiness, and for their pursuit of
the high call of God.*

ACKNOWLEDGMENTS

I WANT TO PERSONALLY thank my daughter, Chanel Sheba Berhane (Hadassah), daughter of the most high God, for typing, editing, and helping me put this book together. Daughter, you help me to fulfill a vital part of my call in the Earth. And my son, Tyrone Berhane, for standing by me through the rough times we have had. Thank you!

With a grateful heart, I wish to acknowledge the team efforts of the excellent staff at Creation House, especially Allen Quain, Virginia Maxwell, and Lauren Simonic. Blessings upon blessings to all of you.

With a heart of honor to whom honor is due, I wish also to acknowledge a good friend of mine, Prophetess Choo Thomas, the author of *Heaven Is So Real* for her efforts to make this book happen.

CONTENTS

ABOUT THE AUTHOR

S HALOM! MY NAME is Asfaw D. Berhane. I was born in the northern part of Ethiopia, where the ark of the covenant is believed to be. I was born into a Jewish family. My father was an Ethiopian Jew named Falasha, who was also a Supreme Court judge, and my mother was Greek Orthodox. I never witnessed my father practicing Judaism, but my mother came from the Levitical priesthood. I received the Lord Jesus Christ as my personal Savior in 1972 at the age of nineteen at the Full Gospel Believers' Church in Addis Ababa, Ethiopia. And yet, growing up, I never heard the term *born again*. In 1974 I joined Youth With A Mission (YWAM), which is an international ministry founded by Loren Cunningham. I left Ethiopia to study Judaism and Eschatology at the International Apostolic Bible College in Denmark. Right after that I moved to Montreal, Canada, to study business at Concordia University. In 1981, I left Canada and moved to Los Angeles, California, to start my own line of product as a fashion designer. I worked in L.A. until 2001, when the Lord called me to full-time ministry at Trinity Broadcasting Network.

Today I possess a prophetic, apostolic, healing, and deliverance anointing in my life. Fellow ministers call me "Smith Wigglesworth," who was a no-nonsense preacher. I am also an end-time seer, a visionary who sees visions and dreams on a consistent basis. I operate in the boldness of faith and believe all sickness is the work of the devil and that God is a good God. I always say, "I don't like the devil, and he does not like me." I take Holy Communion and anoint myself with oil every day. When I go to bed I expect the Lord to speak to me in dreams, to receive a personal visitation from Him, or for the Holy Spirit to come like a rushing wind— and this does happen. I have been visited by the Lord eleven times, visited by God's angels six times, and have been to heaven four times and hell three times.

When I pray for healing for other people, I operate through the word of knowledge. Sometimes I can see the organ of that person that needs to be healed or I can hear the Holy Spirit telling me the infected organ by name. My life of prayer and intercession averages thirteen hours per day, and I fast on average fifteen to twenty-one days per month. I live only for Christ.

FOREWORD

THERE ARE MANY popular books being sold by the thousands and even millions. They may bring laughs, tears, and good memories for a short time, but they do not change a life forever.

Heaven Is Empty, Hell Is Full by Asfaw Berhane is one of few Christian books that can change one's life eternally—if it is read with the right perspective. This book is an eye-opening revelation for Christians, given by the Lord Jesus through visions, dreams, and prophecies.

Asfaw mentioned to me that he does not seek fame or money by publishing the book. His only purpose is to let today's body of Christ know the heart of Jesus toward them.

This is Jesus' love letter to His own, showing how much He cares for today's Laodicean church. It is a "last knocking" at the door of each heart. If you read the book with His heart, your life will be resurrected. It is fearful to say that heaven is empty and hell is full. However, we all must hear the tearful voice of Jesus Himself toward the last days' church through this unknown and obedient servant of God, Asfaw Berhane. God has a great agenda for His church before His coming back. I pray that you all will be partakers of His kingdom and power and glory soon and forever.

—Pastor Michael Park,
AMI Mission Church
Garden Grove, California

> As many as I love, I rebuke and chasten. Therefore be zealous and repent. Behold, I stand at the door and knock.
>
> —Revelation 3:19–20, NKJV

PREFACE

I N THIS BOOK I will be sharing with you the experiences I had in heaven and hell and my awesome visitation with the living Christ and His angelic beings. Through divine revelation the Lord allowed me to see the activity of the place called heaven.

Often, before the visitation with Christ, I would feel the presence and anointing of God. My body would shake and my spirit would groan. At times I would even be sucked out of the roof of my house and travel in the spirit to wherever the Spirit was taking me. I believe I was in my body during these "trips" because I could see my physical body walking the streets of heaven. Yet I do not know for certain if I was truly in my body or out of my body during these miraculous experiences.

The prophet Ezekiel described many of his visionary experiences as being lifted up by the Spirit.

> The Spirit lifted me up and took me away.
> —Ezekiel 3:14

> The Spirit lifted me up between earth and heaven, and brought me in visions of God to Jerusalem.
> —Ezekiel 8:3

> The Spirit took me up and brought me in a vision by the Spirit of God into Chaldea, to those in captivity.
> —Ezekiel 11:24

> The Spirit lifted me up and brought me into the inner court; and behold, the glory of the Lord filled the temple.
> —Ezekiel 43:5

When the Lord told me I would write for Him a book of my testimonies, I came up with all kinds of excuses, just like Moses did. I argued that English is my second language, I am not good with words, and so on until I read a book by a great apostle of faith, Smith Wigglesworth, of the late 1800s and early 1900s. Wigglesworth said, "Never say *I cannot* if you are filled with the Holy Ghost." That statement helped me understand and realize that this was not going to be my book; it is the Lord's book. I am just a pen. He is the ink. After I had built up confidence in myself, I began to put everything together. I tell you all as I saw it and heard it. Read with an open heart, because herein is a mystery and revelation of heaven.

> Surely the Lord God does nothing, Unless He reveals His secret to His servants the prophets.
> —Amos 3:7

1

FIRST ENCOUNTER WITH
THE LIVING CHRIST

It was October 1972, a Saturday night around ten, when the
Lord appeared to me in my room. I did not know why, but I
felt I needed to read a particular Bible that had been given to
me by my father a few years earlier. I had never read from it until
that night. I opened the book and my eyes rested on Psalm 27:1:
"The Lord is my light and my salvation." Right after I read that
verse the power of God started to flow to my weak body, and I was
strengthened. Up until that moment I had been confined to my bed
for a year, suffering from a semi-coma. I had not eaten solid food
for that entire year, and I would vomit blood from my mouth and
nose. That night I was not yet born again, but I as strength coursed
through me I knelt down on the floor and prayed. Suddenly, a
very bright light shone over my face. I saw the Lord Jesus with
His mighty glory wearing a glistening white robe, full of light and
power. His face and hair were glorious and beautiful.

What happened reminds me now of the Damascus road experience. (See Acts 9:1–9.) I was almost blinded by the light that was
streaming forth from Jesus. It was bright and pure and alive, as
it contained the fullness of heavenly glory. I could hardly look at
Him. I fell on His feet and heard myself repeatedly saying, "Have
mercy on me." He was clothed with a white garment down to His
feet. His hair was as white as snow. His eyes were like flames of
fire. His feet were like fine brass refined in a furnace, just as the
Book of Revelation describes. (See Revelation 1:13–17). Shortly
after I was saved and started reading my Bible, I discovered the
Book of Revelation, and John's amazing description of what I had

witnessed unfolded before my eyes. It was a revelation all over again.) The glory that was coming out of His body was so powerful I had to cover my face. Now bear in mind that I had never seen a depiction of Jesus in the natural; I had no idea what He looked like. Yet there was not a trace of doubt in my mind that the being before me was Jesus.

The next morning a friend of my family brought me to church. There I received Christ as my Lord and personal Savior and I was delivered from the spirit of infirmity that had confined me to bed for a year. When the pastor laid his hands on me, I felt lifted up from my body as I was delivered from demonic oppression. My conversion was a miracle, and my family still talks about it, saying, "a dead man came to life."

Since the first time the Lord appeared to me in 1972, He has visited me ten other times. I have been to heaven four times, hell three times, and I have been visited by God's angels six times.

In this book I am going to share my experiences and tell it as I saw it and heard it—nothing more, nothing less. I take this very seriously and ask you to consider this warning:

> For I testify to everyone who hears the words of the prophecy of this book: If anyone adds to these things, God will add to him the plagues that are written in this book; and if anyone takes away from the words of the book of this prophecy, God shall take away his part from the Book of Life, from the holy city, and from the things which are written in this book.
>
> —Revelation 22:18–19

This book is the account of a number of revelations and encounters I have had with the living Christ and angelic beings. Heaven is real; so is hell. I have been to both places. The revelation and experiences that I describe in this book are told just as they happened to me. The purpose of this book is to give the Master, the Lord Jesus Christ, the glory that He deserves. This book will give you hope, for Christ is "the hope of glory" (Col.

1:27). So please read it with an open mind and heart and let the Holy Spirit witness to you.

> The Spirit Himself bears witness with our spirit that we are children of God.
>
> —Romans 8:16

It takes more than a desire to fulfill the will of God. It takes spiritual strength. As you read this book, allow the Spirit of God to point out the areas in your life that need to be focused on or subdued. Then determine that your life and ministry will be a spiritual success.

I am only including part of the mysteries of heaven that God showed me. I can only tell you what I saw, for the mysteries were revealed to me only in part. There are also some things the Lord showed me that I am not allowed to share with anyone. The Bible says:

> The secret things belong to the Lord our God, but those things which are revealed belong to us and to our children forever.
>
> —Deuteronomy 29:29

2

REVELATION OF HEAVEN

ONE MORNING AT three o'clock the Spirit of the Lord lifted me up, supernaturally transporting me from my home. I found myself standing inside one of the magnificent gates of heaven. I was amazed at the indescribable beauty of God's creation. I saw the walls of the city made with precious stones and glittering diamonds. As I stood watching, I was overwhelmed by the experience of being in that glorious place. A multitude wearing white robes were coming to where I was standing. They were praising the Lord.

Leading the multitude were children between the ages of seven and twelve. They were also wearing white robes and glorifying the Lord. Suddenly, the melodies of praise filled the whole atmosphere. Music was above me, around me, and even coming out of the ground. Music after powerful music, worship after powerful worship, praise after powerful praise seemed to penetrate my soul. I couldn't help but join the great multitude by lifting my hands to praise the Lord of glory. The music was like a symphony worshiping in unison. But it was music unlike anything I had ever heard before in my life.

The place I saw was gloriously beautiful. Its wonders are beyond human reasoning or description. The indescribable splendor of that beautiful place called heaven is wondrous to behold; all the brilliance of the light of the Lord Jesus Christ reflecting off the walls of jasper, the pearl gate, the mansions, the river of life, the trees of life, the glassy sea of crystal, the waterfall cascading in a rainbow of many colors. I saw green grass and beautiful gardens. There were colors in heaven that I have never seen before in my life. You can see through them. They look like they can speak to you. I saw blues, reds, greens, yellows, and purples that are nowhere near the colors on Earth. I cannot accurately describe them to you.

Next I found myself standing inside a beautiful pond. There were many distinguished looking people standing still, quietly worshiping the Lord. As I was standing in the pond a bright light was shining on my face. The light was coming from the altar. It grew brighter and brighter, and I was sucked into that massive energy to where the Lord was standing.

There was Jesus, standing with His arms stretched like a cross. I saw the Lord with His brilliant white robes and a massive energy flowing from His body. His piercing eyes were gazing upon me. I saw His virtues begin to flow into my body. I was under His mighty anointing and my body started to vibrate. I knew I was in that secret place of the holy of holies. It reminded me of when "Jesus took Peter, James and John with him and led them up a high mountain, where they were all alone. [And] there he was transfigured before them" (Mark 9:2, NIV). "His face shone like the sun, and his clothes became as white as the light. Just then there appeared before them Moses and Elijah, talking with Jesus" (Matt. 17:2–3, NIV). What I felt was like that glorious experience of old; when I was sucked into that massive energy and consumed by the consuming fire.

> For our God is a consuming fire.
> —Hebrews 12:29

HEAVEN FULL OF WORSHIP

One morning as I was sitting on my couch, thinking about the goodness of the Lord, I suddenly heard the sound of a rushing, mighty wind. The sound filled the room and I saw the wind of the Spirit blowing over my body. I could see a physical wind, not spiritual, shaking my body. I was then sucked out and carried away through the roof of my house.

I immediately found myself in what resembled a golf cart. The angel that was assigned to me was in it. We began to travel down through mountains and valleys and then higher up through the atmosphere of heaven at a faster speed. The vehicle had no doors, it was open, and I was wearing a seat belt. The angel told me to wrap my arms around his neck as we went downhill. I did so and would not let him go. He noticed I was afraid because I was slipping away from my seat.

Finally I found myself standing inside the gate of heaven. I could see inside what looked like a city with paved streets. What I saw and heard was saturated with music, praise, and worship. Heavenly music was everywhere. Everything was in perfect harmony. Music and more music, wave after wave, wonderful anthems of praise were heard everywhere.

Next I saw walls on my left and right. They were constructed of diamonds and precious stones of many colors. I saw glory and power coming out of them. I saw the precious stones on the walls of the pearl gate speak the praises and worship in that part of heaven. The gems were praising the King of Glory. They looked like they could actually see you, and they were responding to the praises of God. They looked like they could speak to you, and they too were worshiping the Lord. They seemed to have life. Everything I saw in heaven has life, and everything praises the Lord.

Heaven is a very busy place. The people I saw, the jasper wall, the worship, the music, the angels of God, and the atmosphere are saturated with the most beautiful worship and praise and music you would ever want to hear. It was as though the grandest symphony orchestra and the most splendid choir ever assembled were performing. It was glorious. I found my being dancing with the music. It was as though every one of my senses were perfectly harmonized with it. My overall sense was one of complete and perfect harmony—of total integration—with everything around me. I was somehow part of it; part of the splendor, part of the harmony, part of the perfection. I was not just seeing and hearing and smelling what was around me; I was integrated into it. I did not just experience joy and love and purity and harmony; I somehow became part of them, and they became part of me. It was the manifestation of the joy, unspeakable joy, of the Holy Spirit. It has been purified and made perfect by the power of almighty God.

> Praise the Lord!
> Sing to the Lord a new song,
> And His praise in the assembly of saints.
> Let Israel rejoice in their Maker;
> Let the children of Zion be joyful in their King.
> Let them praise His name with the dance;
> Let them sing praises to Him with the timbrel and
>   harp. For the Lord takes pleasure in His people;
> He will beautify the humble with salvation.
> Let the saints be joyful in glory;
> Let them sing aloud on their beds.
> Let the high praises of God be in their mouth.
> And a two-edged sword in their hand.
> —Psalm 149:1–6

THE GOLDEN BOWL

An angel of the Lord appeared to me in my home and said, "I have been instructed by the Lord to show you another part of heaven."

Suddenly, I found myself and the angel in what looked like a vehicle, traveling at a phenomenal rate of speed. As we were traveling I saw mountains and hills covered with snow, valleys covered with green grass, and people everywhere. The people had on white gowns and white hats and they looked like they were working or picking up something. When we arrived in another part of paradise, I saw angels coming in and out of those vehicles. They were very busy.

I saw another vehicle zoom in front of me and stop. As the door of that vehicle was opened, I saw a very large blond angel, about ten feet tall, come out and stand by me. He was wearing a brilliant white gown. I saw a large, round golden bowl in his hand. It had some kind of hieroglyphic writing on it. The ten-foot angel handed the golden bowl to another angel. I wondered, "What is this golden bowl?"

> Now when he had taken the scroll, the four living crea-
> tures and the twenty-four elders fell down before the
> Lamb, each having a harp, and golden bowls full of
> incense, which are the prayers of the saints.
>
> —Revelation 5:8

The angel was holding a golden bowl of tears from the earth. The most perfect prayers are those that are prayed through tears; those that come from the heart and soul of men and women on Earth.

Heaven is a very busy place. I saw many angels rushing as if something were about to take place. There were brilliant angels behind me, in front of me, and all around me. They were all blond and beautiful to look at. I noticed some had wings, and they all had on white gowns. I tell you, those angels knew something was up. They were descending and ascending, trafficking people from Earth to heaven.

The angels I saw had ranks and were ordered. Whether you have served in the armed forces or not, I'm sure you are acquainted with how the military ranks its enlisted men and officers. In the army, for example, there are generals at the top and then down through colonels, majors, captains, and lieutenants. Enlisted men also may be identified by different ranks and responsibilities.

Do you know that God also ranks angels? In the New Testament, our Lord used a military term once in connection with angels. When Jesus was about to be taken in the garden of Gethsemane, Peter took out a sword and tried to protect the One he had come to love and serve. Jesus said, "Thinkest thou that I cannot now pray to my Father, and he shall presently give me more than twelve legions of angels?" (Matt. 26:53, KJV) The word *legion* was a Roman military designation referring to about six thousand soldiers.

I saw angels receiving orders from other angels in rank and order. For example, the categories of angels, their names, and rank are:

- Cherubim at the top (Gen. 3:23–24)
- Seraphim (Isa. 6:1–2)
- Living creatures (Rev. 4:8)
- Michael (Dan. 10:13)
- Gabriel (Luke 1:19)
- Lucifer (Isa. 14:12), and so on.

The ten-foot angel I saw was in charge of the other angels there. I also saw angels in military uniform. There is order in heaven.

DISOBEDIENT CHRISTIANS

I saw a large tent that was divided into two sections, one on my left and another on my right. I saw men and very few women in it. The people were all standing with their heads bowed. The men were wearing tan or sandy-colored clothes and the women had colored veils on their heads. The ones on the left side of the tent had on shorts, but the ones on the right side of the tent were wearing long pants. In between these two sections was a path. I saw many angels passing through; some were in those heavenly vehicles zooming to and fro. The people I saw standing in the tent looked sad; they looked lost. I wondered who these people were and what they were doing there.

The Lord later revealed to me that "these were the disobedient Christians waiting for the day of judgment." They were the luke-warm Christians. At that time, the Lord also showed me a pastor being tormented in hell. He had been the pastor of a denominational church, but he did not live right and believed speaking in tongues was of the devil. I urge you, brothers and sisters, living holy isn't something we should only do on Sundays; it is a lifelong choice we are making of either heaven or hell. There is only one answer.

This is a wake-up call message I am sending you from heaven, from the King of Glory.

> Then he [the rich man] said, "I beg you therefore, father, that you would send [Lazarus] to my father's house, for I have five brothers, that he may testify to them, lest they also come to this place of torment." Abraham said to him, "They have Moses and the prophets; let them hear them."
>
> —Luke 16:27–29

There is no time to waste; Jesus is coming soon. Let me ask you this, Are you prepared for eternal life or eternal damnation? We have to make a choice: heaven or hell. The Bible gives us a choice:

> I call heaven and earth as witnesses today against you, that I have set before you life and death, blessing and cursing; therefore choose life, that both you and your descendants may live.
>
> —Deuteronomy 30:19

Brother, sister, if you do not live right you will end up like those people the Lord showed me. You do not want to go there. I have seen the place the Lord prepared for His children—it is called heaven. It is beautiful; it is a breathtaking. But only the ones with pure hearts can enter the kingdom of heaven.

> Who may ascend into the hill of the Lord? Or who may stand in His holy place? He who has clean hands and a pure heart, Who has not lifted up his soul to an idol, Nor sworn deceitfully.
>
> —Psalm 24:3–4

Waterfalls of Many Colors in Heaven

On one of my trips to heaven, the Spirit of the Lord lifted me up and sat me in a place called paradise. In this part of paradise there are bodies of water, trees, waterfalls of many colors, green grass, and flowers. I saw the river of life and trees of life in that fair land. Everything I saw was bright and colored with the brightest colors my eyes had ever beheld. This brilliance was so powerful, no earthly human could take it in. Unless a person has personally witnessed it, his mind has no concept of the glory, beauty, and wonder of what I saw.

In this part of heaven I saw a gate that led me to the sea of glass. It was an endless scene. It looked like glass or the frozen pond of an ice-skating rink. It was beautiful. What thrilled my soul was the magnificent waterfalls of many transparent colors in that part of paradise. The water itself was crystal clear, but of many colors. You could see through the colors. I saw white, red, yellow, green, blue, purple, and many neon colors in the water running down to that paradise. It was a waterfall of many rainbows. The colors on Earth cannot be compared to these colors. The waterfall speaks to you of the wonders of the Lord and declares His glory. The water looks like it can see you.

The environment was saturated with the most beautiful gardens teeming with life. What glorious company there is in heaven. Jesus is there, angels are there, saints are there, music and worship are there. Do not miss heaven. Heaven is so real.

The Painters Paint in Heaven

As I was surveying the waterfalls, the river of life, the trees of life, the flowers, the ocean, and everything else in that paradise, the Spirit of the Lord spoke to my heart. He told me to paint the waterfall of many colors. I saw a white wall in front of me. I started painting, but I did not have any paint or brushes.

I would look at the waterfall of many colors and register it in my mind and then transfer it on to the wall by just thinking of it. There on the wall would appear an original copy of the original.

My "painting" had life. Each shade of color had eyes that could look at you and communicate with you spiritually. The paint moved and flowed like an ocean wave. It had life. It is difficult to explain it properly.

Right after I finished painting the waterfall, I walked up to the higher ground of that paradise and looked down at the paint. It was no longer paint but another waterfall of many colors flowing down to that paradise. I saw both the waterfalls running side by side and flowing into the river of life. It was breathtaking. The music, the worship, the praise, and the magnificent celestial splendor of heaven overwhelmed me. The blazes of His glory, which seemed to shoot from everything I saw, filled me with awe. Brothers and sisters, it excites me to testify of my beautiful visit to heaven. I am thrilled to tell you of the things I saw. Heaven is real and ready. Are you?

LITTLE CHILDREN IN HEAVEN

In one of my visits to heaven, I found myself among a group of children standing in front of one of the ponds. We were all lifting up our hands praising the Lord. Heaven was wide open. The glory of God was shining over the place we were standing. The children and I were surrounded by bright light and filled with the Lord's glory.

There was music playing. There are sounds in heaven that are heard here on Earth as the anointed praises of God. But there is also music in heaven that has never been heard on Earth. The music literally comes out of the ground. It was everywhere. It seems like symphony all together. The music sounds like words, like it is speaking the praises of God.

I saw a blond angel wearing a white gown coming out from the white palace. He said to me, "The Lord wants to have a midnight supper with you." He then went back to the palace. The Lord of glory wants to have a midnight supper with His servant; what a blessing that is for the Lord to say that to you. The children and I continued praising the Lord. I heard the children saying, "I am hungry. I am hungry." I said to them, "Let me go to the pond to see if the food is ready." When I went into the magnificent palace I saw very distinguished people sitting around an oval shaped mahogany table discussing the Word of God. As I was walking through, gazing at the magnificent palace, I saw a room filled with golden-brown steaks and all kind of foods. When I told the children about the food, they started rejoicing with the same expressions of excitement the children in earth use. There is food to eat in heaven. Heaven looks like earth, but thousands of times better.

Children and the Oracles of God

Assuredly, I say to you, unless you are converted and become as little children, you will by no means enter the kingdom of heaven. Therefore whoever humbles himself as this little child is the greatest in the kingdom of heaven.

—Matthew 18:3–4

On my visits to heaven, I saw many children everywhere praising God. There were amphitheaters everywhere. Paradise is a place of praise and worship. I saw children enroll in school in that majestic white palace, which is highly guarded by angels. As I was standing at the gate waiting to enter the palace, an angel of the Lord came out with a book in his hand and said to me, "Your name is not in this record book." I said to the angel, "But I have an invitation from the Lord."

Then I heard a loud voice from the pond saying, "Let him in!" The angel of the Lord opened the gate and let me in. When I walked in through that gate I was met by another handsome blond angel who led me to the children's school. The angel later explained to me that my name was registered in another record book. When I entered the palace, I was amazed by the beauty and wonder of what I saw.

The glory of God was eminent. The house was full of God's glory. The walls were filled with glittering diamonds and other precious stones reflecting the Lord's glory. I saw little children by the thousands sitting on small golden chairs in a classroom. They were being taught the admonition and oracles of God. The children were ages four and under. It was a very large and very long classroom, with the glory of the Lord shining in it.

The angel and I started walking side by side through the room. The floor of the classroom was covered with beautiful, large golden leaves. As the angel and I toured the classroom, I saw the little children smiling at me. The glory of God was shining on them and their faces were brilliant. I saw virtue radiating from their clothes, reflecting the glory of God. Every one of them was looking at me with a smile. As the angel and I walked through the classroom, the children and I greeted one another by bowing our heads out of respect and reverence for each other. My head was down the entire time I was in that classroom. I felt so humbled, and I could tell the children were very happy to see me.

When the Lord showed me the lake of fire, and the pit, I did not see any children there. But in heaven I saw children everywhere. One thing I noticed that was different from the other places I had previously visited in heaven was that to enter this children's pond, you have to go to the gate, which is protected by the guardian angels. And your name has to be in the record book.

Mothers, if you have lost children, the Lord has them. Whether you had an abortion or a miscarriage or by natural means your child died, the Lord has him or her. (Read Ezekiel 16.) I even saw three little toddlers fly through the sky and land right in front of me. They were looking and gazing at me with joy. They had on white gowns and they each had wings.

As I am writing this book, I wonder if these three toddlers could be my children. You see, when I was married, my wife and I had three abortions. After I got saved I asked the Lord to forgive me, and He did. One day when I go to heaven I will see them, and you will see yours if you are saved and live a holy life for Jesus. Glory to God!

Ephesians 3:14–16 confirms that there are families in heaven:

> For this reason I bow my knees to the Father of our Lord
> Jesus Christ, from whom the whole family in heaven and
> earth is named, that He would grant you, according to
> the riches of His glory, to be strengthened with might
> through His Spirit in the inner man.

GOLDEN, HEAVENLY RAIN

One morning at three o'clock I was before the Lord seeking His
face and pouring out my heart before Him. Suddenly the power of
the Holy Spirit shook my body violently and lifted me up, carrying
me away to heaven. I found myself in a large complex surrounded
by a group of saints. These redeemed saints were conversing about
the kingdom of God. One of the saints handed me a book. With
the book in my hand, I left the building and started walking
through the gardens of that paradise. I observed one light blue,
brand-new eighteen-wheeler driving very slowly down the street
of that paradise. It was similar to the gasoline trucks we see on
Earth, but there was no driver in it.

As I was walking along the street of heaven, it began to rain. It
rained and rained and rained. But the rain was not like the rain
we see on Earth; this heavenly rain was not wet at all. The drops
were like drops of pure crystal light or like small diamonds that
had light and life inside them. They fell so softly and smoothly
from above, like glitter. Wherever I went, the rain followed me.
I was encircled by the pleasurable drops. They were very light
and airy.

Next I saw a group of female worshipers standing and praising
the Lord in the middle of that glistening land. I joined hands with
two of them and began praising God. Then I saw myself continue
walking in that paradise. A mighty, rushing wind lifted me up
and carried me away inside a palace. My body started shaking
and groaning as the Holy Spirit was working on me. While this
was happening, I could see myself from outside my body. I was

praising in the spirit and speaking in tongues as the power of the Holy Spirit was shaking my body. It was a glorious experience in that place called heaven.

> When He utters His voice—There is a multitude of waters in the heavens: "He causes the vapors to ascend from the ends of the earth; He make lightnings for the rain; He brings the wind out of His treasuries."
> —Jeremiah 51:16

SILENCE IN HEAVEN: HOLY OF HOLIES

> When He opened the seventh seal, there was silence in heaven for about half an hour. I saw the seven angels who stand before God, and to them were given seven trumpets. Then another angel, having a golden censer, came and stood at the altar. He was given much incense, that he should offer it with the prayers of all the saints upon the golden altar which was before the throne. And the smoke of the incense, with the prayers of the saints, ascended before God from the angel's hand. Then the angel took the censer, filled it with fire from the altar, and threw it to the earth. And there were noises, thunderings, lightnings, and an earthquake. So the seven angels who had the seven trumpets prepared themselves to sound.
> —Revelation 8:1–6

On one of my visits to heaven, I was taken to a particular place where I had an experience with the living Christ in the holy of holies. The Lord and a great many angels were assembled in that magnificent and majestic temple. It was the temple of the Lord filled with His glory. I saw the Lord standing by the altar. He was wearing a white silk robe with gold embroidery. I saw a great many angels standing still all around the temple. I was standing right behind the Lord.

There was silence in heaven. Everything in that holy of holies was breathtaking. The Lord Himself was standing still, praying. Then I saw three white suits, folded neatly, and laying on the altar in front of the Lord and me. All the angels were standing in awe. As I watched this scene, somehow I knew these three suits were for me to wear as I served in my ministry. Amazed, I questioned to myself, "Why three white suits?" Then I realized three is the number of divinity and the color white symbolizes purity and perfection.

In the past, I had dreams of me wearing a white suit while I was preaching. In my dreams it seemed I was in the temple of God for an hour, standing still in the presence of God almighty and His mighty angels. Habakkuk 2:20 tells us, "But the Lord is in His holy temple. Let all the earth keep silence before Him." The Lord of heaven and Earth brought me from Earth to the destination of righteousness, beyond the atmosphere and starry skies into the temple of God, the holy of holies—into the immediate presence of God.

Heaven is the dwelling place of God. In Psalm 11:4 it is called God's holy temple and a place where His throne is. I was there in the temple of God's divine majesty. His excellent glory is revealed in the most conspicuous manner. There is order. There is silence and stillness, only the glory of the Lord speaks to us Spirit to spirit. It was a sacred place full of light, joy, and glory. Jesus was the center focus of the saints, angels, and all the worshiping beings standing behind the King of Glory.

Brothers and sisters, it excites me to testify of my glorious visit to heaven. I am thrilled to tell you of the things I saw. Saints, the radiant, magnificent, celestial splendor of heaven overwhelmed me. The beauty and bliss of heaven cannot accurately be pictured by the mind's eye unless a person has seen it for himself.

The City of New Jerusalem

The Spirit of the Lord lifted me up and sat me by a high mountain. I climbed higher and higher to the top of the mountain. On the other side of the mountain, I saw hills, waters, valleys, and a narrow road. I began to walk down the hills on the narrow road.

Suddenly I was riding a white horse. The horse was beautiful, gentle, humble, and very peaceful. He was as white as snow and the largest, tallest, healthiest stallion I have ever seen in my life. The horse started moving slowly at first and then began to pick up speed as he galloped through the valley. He maneuvered along the winding hills and roads at an even greater speed.

Abruptly I saw the road merge into a sea of water. The horse continued moving on top of the sea. It was a glorious and smooth ride on the ocean. It felt like the Spirit of the Lord was carrying us away. After miles and miles on top of the ocean, I was lifted up from the top of the horse by the Spirit of God. I saw myself flying higher and higher, mounting up with wings like an eagle. It felt like I was traveling for hours; I saw nothing but atmosphere. I looked below me and in front of me, but there was nothing but empty space. I could see and feel the tangible, mighty, physical power of the wind of the Holy Spirit carrying me away.

Then I saw from a distance what appeared to be a green island that was the size of a football field. As I got closer and closer, the island grew bigger and bigger. The closer I moved, the more intense, alive, and vivid everything became. It was the city of new Jerusalem. As I reached the city, my senses were even more heightened, and I felt deliriously happy. I was thrilled at the prospect of seeing this place, so I attempted to land. I knew everything would be even more thrilling than what I had experienced so far. During that momentary pause, the Spirit of the Lord would not allow me to land.

As I was wondering why, I heard the still small voice saying, "You've been inside the city, now you are seeing it from above." The city glowed like a great light before me. The light shone with the radiance of many stars and everything I saw in that glorious city was beautiful and alive. This was the new Jerusalem, the city of God laying in splendor before me. To fly in an airplane is one thing, but flying in the spirit is another. I have experienced it many times.

Now I saw heaven opened, and behold a white horse. And He who sat on him was called Faithful and True, and in righteousness He judges and makes war. His eyes were like a flame of fire, and on His head were many crowns. He had a name written that no one knew except Himself. He was clothed with robe dipped in blood, and His name is called The Word of God. And the armies in heaven, clothed in fine linen, white and clean, followed Him on white horses. Now out of His mouth goes a sharp sword, that with it He should strike the nations and He Himself will rule them with the rod of iron, He Himself treads the winepress of the fierceness and wrath of Almighty God. And He Has on His robe and on His thigh a name written: KING OF KINGS AND LORD OF LORDS.

—Revelation 19:11–16

OPEN HEAVENS: THE THRONE OF GOD

After these things I looked, and behold, a door standing open in heaven. And the first voice which I heard was like a trumpet speaking with me, saying, "Come up here, and I will show you things which must take place after this." Immediately I was in the Spirit; and behold, a throne set in heaven, and One sat on the throne. And He who sat there was like a jasper and a sardius stone in appearance; and there was a rainbow around the throne, in appearance like an emerald. Around the throne were twenty-four thrones, and on the thrones I saw twenty-four elders sitting, clothed in white robes; and they had crowns of gold on their heads. And from the throne proceeded lightnings, thunderings, and voices. Seven lamps of fire were burning before the throne, which are the seven Spirits of God. Before the throne there was a sea of glass, like crystal. And in the midst of the throne,

and around the throne, were four living creatures full of
eyes in front and in back.

—Revelation 4:1–6

On June 18, 2007, at 8:00 a.m., I had just risen from my bed
and was sitting on the couch. I started feeling something. I could
sense something was up, a compulsion. I did not know why I
was picking up in the spirit that something was going on in the
spirit realm. I felt I needed to stand up and praise the Lord.

The more I praised Him, the stronger the anointing grew. My
hands and my body grew weaker and weaker. My entire body
was vibrating violently. I could no longer lift my arms. My body
slowly started to give up, and I was slain in the spirit. I saw a
vivid and powerful vision of the open heaven. A beam of fire
proceeded from my eyes and started shooting into the sky. The
beam of fire was traveling at a high speed. I could see with my
own eyes a literal fire.

The beam of fire started extending as it was shooting higher
and higher into the sky. It got bigger and bigger, like fireworks
on the Fourth of July. The beam even whistled like fireworks do
as it was shooting across the sky. Remember, this was happening
to me while I was wide awake. I could see a beam of fire coming
out my two eyes and shooting to the heavenlies with a whistle. I
do not know how to explain it. As the beam was shooting higher
and higher to the sky, the heavens started to open wider, and I
saw the indescribable throne of God with a mighty glory around
it coming out and meeting my eyes. I saw the golden throne
of God and His glory around it. After this open heaven vision
was over, I was just sitting on the couch as I was before. I have
seen visions before, but never as powerful as this one. I was very
much aware of my while this vision was happening. After this
open vision and divine experience, I noticed wherever I went
people would point at me. The glory of the Lord was still strong
on me. Glory to His name.

3

REVELATION OF HELL

Enter by the narrow gate; for wide is the gate and broad is the way that leads to destruction, and there are many who go in by it. Because narrow is the gate and difficult is the way which leads to life, and there are few who find it.

—Matthew 7:13–14

ON MY SECOND visit to heaven, the Lord Jesus brought me back to that gloriously beautiful place called paradise for a brief visit. The overwhelming beauty of what I saw around me was wonderfully breathtaking. As I was walking and enjoying God's creation, I saw the Lord standing a few steps away from me. The Lord did not speak to me, but He motioned with His hand in the direction He wanted me to look.

What I saw was a lake of fire. It was about a quarter of a mile away from where we were standing. Thousands upon thousands of people were in torment, moving up and down in this volcanic lake. There was dark steam rising up from the surface of the lake. The Lord motioned to me again for me to look in the opposite direction at the paradise from which I had just come. There I saw the trees, green grass, and all the beauty of heaven, but I saw only a very few people in it.

The Lord asked me, "What do you see?" I said, "Lord, I see heaven is empty and hell is full." He said, "If my children would follow the great commission I have given them, heaven would not be empty." He continued to say, "There are very few of my generals following my instructions. I want you to follow their footsteps."

Then He showed me a vision of His servants, the prophets. I saw each one of them demonstrating the power of God in a miraculous way. Each one of them laid their hands on me and I fell on the ground under a mighty anointing. I began to praise the Lord in the spirit.

Immediately after this vision, I had another vision. There were two prophetesses of God falling into error. One of the prophetesses was boasting and full of pride. I saw her being judgmental, putting me down, and cursing other fellow ministers of the gospel. She was giving glory to herself. The other prophetess was falling under the error of sexual immorality. She was trying to seduce me and other ministers. I said to myself, "How could this be?" I had seen these two prophetesses on the Christian television network many times.

I was disturbed by what I saw and heard. The vision then disappeared and the Lord reappeared. He said, "I want you to follow the steps of my generals." I said, "Lord! why did you show me the two prophetesses?" He said, "Didn't you read My words that say 'men will be lovers of themselves'?" I said, "Yes, Lord, it is in 2 Timothy 3:2." The Lord answered, "I do not share My glory with anyone." And He vanished. Let us read 2 Timothy 3:2–4:

> For men will be lovers of themselves, lovers of money, boasters, proud, blasphemers, disobedient to parents, unthankful, unholy, unloving, unforgiving, slanderers, without self-control, brutal, despisers of good, traitors, headstrong, haughty, lovers of pleasure rather then lovers of God.

Since the Lord showed me the vision of the Katrina flood, the flood in the land of Ethiopia, and the two prophetesses, which are described in this book, they have all come to pass, with the exception of one of the prophetesses.

None of you can be strong in God unless you diligently hearken to what God has to say to you through His Word. You cannot know the power and the nature of God unless you partake of His inbreathed Word.

The psalmist said that he hid God's Word in his heart, that he might not sin against Him (Ps. 119:11). You will find that the more of God's Word you hide in your heart, the easier it is to live a holy life. The psalmist also testified that God's Word had quickened him (see vv. 50, 93); and as you receive God's Word into your being, your whole physical being will be quickened and you will be made strong. As you receive the Word with meekness, faith will spring up within you. You will have life through the Word. Do not give the devil a place in your life. Remember, whenever you read the Word, the Word is reading you. It is a mirror of your life.

> Surely the Lord God does nothing, Unless He reveals His secret to His servants the prophets. A lion has roared! Who will not fear? The Lord God has spoken! Who can but prophesy?
>
> —Amos 3:7–8

Brothers and sisters, what a designation for any person—"My generals"! God was identifying Himself with His servants the prophets. Thank God for their faithfulness.

LESSONS TO BE LEARNED

Dear brothers and sisters, no one by any means is judging anyone. "For whom the Lord loves He chastens" (Heb. 12:6). This is a lesson for every Christian to learn from the mistakes of our past and also to learn from God's generals why some succeeded and why some failed. Alexander Dowie, the healing apostle of the late 1800s who was used by God in a mighty way, fell into error. Eventually Dowie so sadly diverted from God's plan for his life that he embraced the suggestion that he was Elijah and proclaimed it as truth.

William Branham is another man of God known as a man of notable signs and wonders. But Branham, like Alexander Dowie, turned to radical doctrine and sensationalism. Here are some of his doctrines. In his last days, Branham taught no eternal hell. He said hell was forever, but not for eternity. *Forever* for him meant a period of time. After that period of time, those in hell would be annihilated. He also taught that women weren't created by God but were merely a by-product of man. He even suggested that animals were a higher rank of species than women because they were created from nothing. According to Branham, women are the most easily deceived and despiteful beings on Earth. Branham also taught that women carry the seed of the serpent. This doctrine taught that Eve and the serpent had sexual relations in the garden and created Cain. According to Branham every woman carries the literal seed of the devil. Branham once said, "Every time that a funeral goes down the street a woman caused it." He also said that women have to be punished, so men can have many wives, but women only one husband. Branham taught that when Jesus spoke on divorce, He was speaking to the woman, not the man. A woman could not remarry under any circumstances. But a man could divorce whenever he wanted to and remarry a virgin.

How could a man used by God turn to radical doctrine? The stories of Alexander Dowie, William Branham, and the two prophetesses the Lord showed me were not written for criticism. I believe they contain a lesson more powerful than this one chapter can hold. The lesson here is this: do what God says to do, nothing more and nothing less. There is no game here. There is one move, and it belongs to God. Your job is to follow it. You are either in the will of God or out of it. All Branham and Dowie wanted was to be a voice. If they had remained in the plan of God, they could have been the greatest voices that had ever lived. Thank God for Smith Wigglesworth, Billy Graham, Jack Hayford, Oral Roberts, and many others of God's generals for their faithfulness, loyalty, trustworthiness, and their pursuit to reach the high call of God.

We must understand that great error comes from not having both the Word and the Spirit working together in one's life. Never deviate from it because of your own ideas or pressure from others. Your anointing or calling will only come when you follow the plan that God has outlined for you, so embrace that plan and hold to it tightly. Then, run strong with it and do mighty exploits, in Jesus' name.

THE BRINK OF HELL: THIRTY MINUTES OF TORMENT

The Spirit of the Lord lifted me up and sat me in a transporter-like vehicle. There was neither a seat in the car nor any doors on it. I had to stand and hold on to a handrail. The transporter was traveling through a very narrow channel between an ocean of pure water on one side, which was flowing to paradise, and a deep, dark pit full of tormented spirits on the other side. The channel was a great fixed gulf. On either side there was either the endless river or the endless pit. When I looked over paradise, I would feel peace for just a second. When I looked over the deep dark pit I would feel tormented from the force that was coming out the pit. The ride through the channel was over thirty minutes long. Thirty minutes of torment came from the evil force in the dark, deep pit. I could hear noises, shouting coming from the pit; the sounds were almost pulling me down into the darkness. I would not wish for anyone to experience the fear and the torment that was surrounding me. After thirty minutes of being around the pit, the transporter brought me back to paradise, where I finally felt relief. I had traveled through the gulf that separated hell and heaven, where Lazarus and the rich man were.

> There was a certain rich man who was clothed in purple and fine linen and fared sumptuously every day. But there was a certain beggar named Lazarus, full of sores, who was laid at his gate, desiring to be fed with the crumbs which fell from the rich man's table. Moreover the dogs came and licked his sores. So it was that the beggar died, and was carried by the angels to Abraham's bosom. The rich man also died and was buried. And being in torments in Hades, he lifted up his eyes and saw Abraham afar off, and Lazarus in his bosom. Then he

27

cried and said, "Father Abraham, have mercy on me, and send Lazarus that he may dip the tip of his finger in water and cool my tongue; for I am tormented in this flame." But Abraham said, "Son, remember that in your lifetime you received your good things, and likewise Lazarus evil things; but now he is comforted and you are tormented. And besides all this, between us and you there is a great gulf fixed, so that those who want to pass from here to you cannot, nor can those from there pass to us." Then he said, "I beg you therefore, father, that you would send him to my father's house, for I have five brothers, that he may testify to them, lest they also come to this place of torment." Abraham said to him, "They have Moses and the prophets; let them hear them." And he said, "No, father Abraham; but if one goes to them from the dead, they will repent." But he said to him, "If they do not hear Moses and the prophets, neither will they be persuaded though one rise from the dead."

—Luke 16:19–31

The Smoking Pit

After a brief visit to heaven, the Holy Spirit led me to a different area outside the kingdom. I walked and walked through a vast, dry and burned land until I came to a narrow, winding street. The street led to an underground building with an iron gate. The gate was about sixteen feet high and about fifty feet wide. As I was standing, gazing, and wondering what this underground place was doing in the middle of the wilderness, I saw the gate opening upward. A dark cloud of smoke filled the entrance. I could see deep into the smoking pit as a billowing cloud rose up like steam. The frightening scene smelled like sulfur.

As I was standing and gazing at the pit opening before me, my attention was directed toward a figure that was coming out of the pit to stand at the gate. The figure was my mother. She looked at me and said, "Asfaw! Do not come to this place! Do not come to this place!" I saw my own mother warning me not to go to that tormenting place called hell. Right after she said that, my mother turned her back to me and disappeared into the deep, smoky pit. The gate then closed downward.

My mother died in 1994. I had not seen her since I left Ethiopia in 1974. She looked the same as I had remembered her. My mother was a beautiful and good woman. She was raised in the Greek Orthodox Church. In fact, her father was a high priest. My mother knew about Jesus, but she did not know Him as her personal Savior.

I don't believe the Lord showed me my mother in hell to hurt me. He showed her to me so that I would be able to tell others that no matter how good you are or what your religious affiliation is, unless you are born again and live a holy life you will by no means enter the kingdom of God. Only those who have a pure heart and are faithful to Him are going to see Him. Let me ask you this, Do you know Him? Do you know where you going? Are you Rapture-ready? Do not be left behind. Heaven is real, and so is hell.

4

VISITATION FROM THE LORD

Therefore do not worry, saying, "What shall we eat?" or "What shall we drink?" or "What shall we wear?" For after all these things the Gentiles seek. For your heavenly Father knows that you need all these things. But seek first the kingdom of God and His righteousness, and all these things shall be added to you.
—**Matthew 6:31–33**

WHEN THE LORD called me into full-time ministry, I began to worry. I had been a fashion designer for over eighteen years. I remember thinking, "How am I going to support myself and my children if I have to give up my business?" I said, "Lord, if You will take care of me and my children, I will serve you full time. You know, Lord, I am a single parent and I do not have any family here."

A week later, an angel of the Lord came to my house and brought me outside to where my truck was parked. He started wiping and polishing my truck with a cloth in his hand. I remembered that I had once asked the Lord to keep my truck in good shape because the place where He called me to minister was about sixty miles (one way) from my home. I was worried about the wear on my truck. As the angel was cleaning my truck, I saw it become brand-new again. I asked the angel why he was doing this, and He pointed his finger to where the Lord was standing.

I saw the Lord in His glory with His hands raised to heaven. He was praying. I saw heaven open. The glory coming out of the Lord's body covered the whole area where He was standing. I heard music. Worship was descending from heaven followed by radiant light shining over the place where the Lord was standing. His glory was all over the place. I looked back at the angel who escorted me. He was six feet tall, blond, and very handsome. He was wearing a fine white robe. Then the Lord disappeared.

The angel of the Lord said, "I have been instructed by the Lord to take care of you, your children, and your ministry." He said, "There is no need to worry." At the time of this writing, it has been five years since this encounter. I have never been broke since. My family has had more than enough, and I am very grateful to the Lord for what He has been doing for me and my children. I am ministering under prophetic, apostolic, and healing anointings. Praise the Lord forevermore. My children are in college. They love the Lord and are born again.

By the way, since the Lord called me to full-time ministry five years ago, I have traveled with the same truck over 180,000 miles without any measure of problems. She's still running smooth.

INSTRUCTED TO PRAY IN TONGUES

The Spirit of the Lord carried me away in the spirit and sat me on a high mountain. I found myself sitting on a large rock overlooking a vast land. There was nothing but flat land as far as my eyes could see. As I was wondering why I was there, I suddenly heard someone praying in tongues. When I turned to see where the voice was coming from, I saw the Lord Jesus in His Shekinah glory praying in tongues. His head was covered and He was wearing a white robe. He was sitting on a large rock, which was similar to the one I was sitting on, and it was covered with the brilliance of His glory. He said, "I am giving you a special gift of tongues." He instructed me to pray in tongues more often. Since that day, my prayer has been in the Spirit, in tongues.

> Likewise the Spirit also helps in our weaknesses. For we do not know what we should pray for as we ought, but

the Spirit Himself makes intercession for us with groanings which cannot be uttered.

—Romans 8:26

The Lord was sharing His secret with His servant. Paul understood the power of praying in the Spirit. Paul said, "I wish you all spoke with tongues....I speak with tongues more than you all" (1 Cor. 14:5, 18). When we pray in tongues we are speaking directly to the Lord. Our heart must be cheerful and clean in order to experience His presence and to hear His voice. When I am in prayer and enter into His presence, my body starts shaking and my spirit groans. There is power in praying in the Spirit.

THE KING OF KINGS, LORD OF LORDS

When the Lord called me into full-time ministry in 2001, I began to see angels, demons, colors, oceans, lights, mountains, rivers, multitudes, visions, and dreams on a regular and consistent basis.

Once, Jesus and I were standing behind a great multitude as they were entering into a temple. These were the redeemed Christians. Jesus was wearing a white, glorious robe that hung to His feet. He looked to be about six feet tall. Virtue was coming out His body. I saw writing on His chest: "KING OF KINGS, LORD OF LORDS."

He looked at me and said, "You will bring Me souls just like the people you see in front of you." As Jesus was saying this, He seemed to be proud of His redeemed children. I said, "Lord, I have wasted half of my life serving the devil."

He replied, "I will redeem the time you lost." Suddenly, I saw a vision of myself. I was outside my body watching as my body transformed into a hundred-year-old body that still looked young. I asked the Lord, "Why am I having dreams and visions on a regular and consistent basis?" He answered, "My son, you are an end-time seer."

What is a seer? Jim Gull, who is a seer himself, explains in his book *The Seer*, "Within the overall realm of the prophet lies the particular and distinctive realm of the Seers." The word *seer* describes a particular prophet who receives a particular type of prophetic revelation. Gull goes on to say:

> All true seers are prophets, but not all prophets are seers. Seers are gifted to see angels, demons, lights, colors, and dreams and visions. A seer is a prophet. The distinction between a prophet and a seer is that a prophet is an inspired hearer and then speaker, while a seer is visual. A seer's anointing emphasizes visions and the revelatory gifts mingled with the gift of discerning of spirits rather than the audible, speaking gifts. Visual "seeing" involves insights, revelations, warnings, and prophecies from the Spirit of God's revelation while the seer's spirit simply observes and receives the message. To see the Lord in a dream is visual, but for Him to manifest Himself to the person dreaming is actual.

The gift of prophecy involves speaking under the direct supernatural influence of the Holy Spirit. The gift of prophecy is the supernaturally imparted ability to hear the voice of the Holy Spirit and speak God's mind in order to edify, exhort, and comfort.

A Flame of Fire

One evening I was asking the Holy Spirit to reveal Jesus to me. A few weeks later, the Lord, with His mighty glory, appeared to me. I saw Him standing in front of me, and He was filled with His glory.

He did not speak to me. He seemed to be a little taller than I had previously perceived Him. I saw a fire of glory coming out of His body. Glory was radiating from His robe, which looked amber from the flame of fire. I saw that His power, His virtue, and His glory were moving His brilliant robe. It was the wave of His glory moving His garment. I have seen the Lord's garment before, but I've never seen Him with a wave of fire coming out from His robe. We had a heart-to-heart conversation. I said, "Thank you for showing up as I have asked You."

I know the Lord very intimately and I am obsessed with Him. He knows me. He talks to me. He is my best friend. We share everything with each other, and He has never disappointed me. Every morning I say, "Good morning, Father; good morning, Jesus; good morning, Holy Spirit." He responds by saying, "Good morning, Asfaw." If you talk to Him, I promise you He will talk to you. Get closer to Him, and He will get closer to you. Seek Him with all your heart, and you will find Him. Get right with the Lord. He loved you enough to endure the cross for you. His blood is still flowing. There is a mighty power in His blood to clean you from your unrighteousness. No matter what you have done, there is no sin in the pit of hell that the blood of Jesus cannot wash away. He will clean you up. That is what I love about my Jesus. He is my best friend, the man from Galilee.

Do not view yourself as other people see you; focus on how God sees you. You see, brothers and sisters, as we hunger and thirst for God, we move deeper into our relationship with God. Then He starts to unfold His plan for our lives and the work He has for us to do. Be a soldier in God's end-time army. Be a constant flame of fire, continuously burning. This means to have an inward burning of love and compassion, zeal and prayer, and praise. Burning but never burned out; on fire, but never consumed, like the burning bush. The yearning for God brings the burning.

Remember, life in Christ in many ways is a paradox. What is up is actually down. The way to receive is to give. To lose is to gain. Fellowship from suffering comes from experiencing a broken heart. Let Him mold you and break you. Great faith is the product of a great fight. Great testimonies are the result of great testing. Great triumphs come only out of great trials. Every stumbling block can become a stepping stone. Every opposition must become an opportunity.

One time I thought I had the Holy Ghost, but now I know that the Holy Ghost has me. Brothers and sisters, do you know Him? Whenever you walk with God, do not know too much. When you know too much, you will miss it. Play it by ear. Doing God's will is not just doing what is convenient. It is doing what is right, even when *right* is not convenient. Doing God's will often will take you out your comfort zone. To possess the Holy Spirit is one thing, to *be possessed* is another thing. Those who are possessed by the zeal of God are movers and shakers in the kingdom of God. Trust in God and His own Word. Trust in the integrity of God. Step out by faith. God has a plan for your life that He thought out before the foundation of the world.

> Therefore, since we are receiving a kingdom which cannot be shaken, let us have grace, by which we may serve God acceptably with reverence and godly fear. For our God is a consuming fire.
>
> —Hebrews 12:28–29

You Will Build Me a Temple

> "Concerning this temple which you are building, if you walk in My statutes, execute My judgments, keep all My commandments, and walk in them, then I will perform My word with you, which I spoke to your father David. And I will dwell among the children of Israel, and will not forsake My people Israel." So Solomon built the temple and finished it.
>
> —1 Kings 6:12–14

A few months before the vision of which I am about to tell you, a prophetess prophesied the following over me: "You will build Me a temple, and I will give you seven more churches." Shortly after, I received another prophecy from another prophetess of God, which said, "I will build Him seven churches."

Six months later the Lord took me in the spirit to the place where I first encountered the living Christ in 1972. This place is where the ark of the covenant is believed to be, in St. Mary's of Zion Church, which is located in the northern part of Ethiopia. In this vision, the Lord showed me a magnificent building made up of golden bricks. On the top of the roof I saw a group of priests wearing robes of many colors. They were carrying the ark of the covenant on their shoulders and walking and praising God back and forth, from one end of the rooftop to the other. As I was amazed by what was taking place, I heard the still small voice saying, "You will build me Solomon's temple."

A few months passed and I had another vision. In this one, I was back at this place, standing with two other men in front of Solomon's majestic temple. One of the men asked me how long it took to build this magnificent temple. I said, "It took three years for my Father to build the temple," (I was talking about my heavenly Father).

Then the Lord showed me another vision not far from the temple, I saw a large building with many trees around it. The building was in a beautiful complex, which was surrounded by mountains. I heard again that small voice, this time saying, "You will build a Bible school and an orphanage for my children." For many years the Lord would show me dreams of me working with children from around the world. I would pray to the Lord to give me those children. The Book of Isaiah says, "'Whom shall I send, And who will go for Us?' Then I said, 'Here am I! Send me'" (Isa. 6:8).

What about you? Will you say, as Isaiah said, "Here am I, Lord. Send me"? Or are you one of those who keeps on hearing, but does not understand; who keeps on seeing, but does not perceive? This is my prayer: whatever your calling is, you will answer Him with, "Yes! Send me." There is much work to be done in the kingdom of God.

JESUS TRANSFIGURED BEFORE MY EYES

Once, in a vision, I was entering a large complex that looked like a television studio. As I entered the building, I noticed three cameras and a crew standing by to film. I noticed the logos on the cameras were ABC, NBC, and CNN.

As I was making my way to the stage I saw two chairs that were apparently reserved for the guests. Suddenly a man wearing a white suit appeared in one of the chairs. I sat next to him and noticed that I was wearing the same white suit he was wearing. When I turned toward the man to greet him, he was transfigured before my own eyes into the Lord Jesus Himself.

When I looked at Him, His face shone like the sun and His clothes became as white as light. A power and a virtue came out of Him and flowed to my body.

I was sucked in and out, back and forth into His power. My body started shaking violently. I was under tremendous anointing, and I fell against His bosom. This continued for a few minutes, and then I heard the Lord saying, "I am giving you all the networks. Go, preach My gospel." This experience reminded me of when Jesus led Peter, James, and John to the high mountain and was transfigured before them.

> His face shone like the sun, and His clothes became as white as the light. And behold, Moses and Elijah appeared to them, talking with Him.
>
> —Matthew 17:2–3

Saints, it is time to claim what the devil has stolen from us. We have to take over the media for Jesus Christ's sake. "The earth is the Lord's, and all its fullness" (Ps. 24:1). Whatever the devil meant for harm, the Lord is going to turn for good. Christians have been ridiculed by the secular media for so long. It is time for us to ridicule the devil and take over what he has stolen from us. The gospel must be preached to the ends of the world. The people "limited the Holy One of Israel" (Ps. 78:41). Do not limit God, the unlimited God of Israel.

I Have Given You the World

> Go into all the world and preach the gospel to every creature. He who believes and is baptized will be saved; but

he who does not believe will be condemned. And these
signs will follow those who believe: In My name they will
cast out demons; they will speak with new tongues; they
will take up serpents; and if they drink anything deadly,
it will by no means hurt them; they will lay hands on the
sick, and they will recover.

—Mark 16:15–18

Every morning at 3:00 a.m. the Lord wakes me up for prayer.
I drop to my knees to hear what the Lord had to say for that
particular day. During one of these early morning prayer sessions,
I noticed a light flickering in the room. It then began to spread
across the floor.

I jumped up from my prayers and noticed a ball of fire shining
on the wall of my room. I then saw the Lord standing on the floor
by the light on the wall. A world map lit up on the wall from
within the ball of fire. I saw six of the seven continents on the
map, with each country's name written on it. I saw Africa, Asia,
Europe, Australia, and North and South America. The vision was
panoramic, like I was watching it on a large movie screen.

As I was looking at each of the continents and the countries
within them, I noticed a large table covered with a white table-
cloth. A Holy Communion and a silver scepter or rod were on
the table. The rod was about 24 inches long and it had some kind
of writing on it. While all this was happening, the Lord was still
standing on the floor by the table. Then the Lord spoke: "What I
am about to show you is what is about to happen in your ministry."
He said, "Pick up the scepter and dip it in my blood (the Holy
Communion) and touch every country that has names written on
it." (There were a few countries with no names written on them.)
I touched every country, as I was told. The Lord said, "Now place
My body (the bread) in every country as they appeared." I picked
up the bread and placed some of it on every country, as I was
instructed. He said, "Now keep the scepter with you at all times. I
have given you the world."

The Lord looked the same as I had previously perceived Him, standing at about six feet tall. He had piercing eyes full of compassion and love. He was wearing a white robe and glory was radiating from His body. Right after the visitation from the Lord, I opened my Bible to see what the Scriptures have to say about scepters:

> A scepter of righteousness is the scepter of Your kingdom. You have loved righteousness and hated lawlessness; Therefore God, Your God, has anointed You With the oil of gladness more than Your companions.
> —Hebrews 1:8–9

Right after the Lord said to me, "I have given you the world," He took me in the spirit to see my future. In a vision He showed me images of myself in churches, in marketplaces, and on the streets laying hands on the sick in Jesus' name. I saw people getting healed. I saw a woman and two men raised from the dead as I commanded the spirit of death to come out and I spoke life to their bodies. I was under a mighty anointing. As I was walking along the streets, I would touch people and they would fall to the ground under the power of God. What an experience that was!

In order to see a demonstration of the hand of God at work, you have to walk with strong compassion and a rock-solid faith in God. A Christian must act upon what he believes in order to receive the manifestation. Faith is just believing. Understand that you are not the healer, God is. Only believe. Do not move by what you see or hear; move by what you believe. Do what Jesus did. Take authority. Speak the Word without doubt, for the Word has power to perform miracles, signs, and wonders:

> And through the hands of the apostles many signs and wonders were done among the people. And they were all with one accord in Solomon's Porch. Yet none of the rest dared join them, but the people esteemed them highly. And believers were increasingly added to the Lord, multitudes of both men and women, so that they brought the

sick out into the streets laid them on beds and couches, that at least the shadow of Peter passing by might fall on some of them.

—Acts 5:12–15

THE GOLDEN BOTTLE

One morning around eight o'clock I returned home from dropping off my children at school. As I sat down on my couch, I started to feel a compulsion. Suddenly, I was caught up in the Spirit. I saw and felt a physical, rushing wind carry me away. I was lifted up and sucked out the roof of my house.

The wind brought me to an open field. There I saw two young black men who were wearing black suits and white shirts. I noticed they were identical twins. I asked them if I could pray for them, and they agreed. As we were holding hands and praying, I saw the twins begin to multiply. The two became four, and then eight, and on and on until there was a great multitude.

Next I saw the Lord and an angel standing before me. The angel had one large golden bottle and one small bottle in his hands. I was bowing on my knees between the Lord and the angel. The angel handed the golden bottle to the Lord, and He poured oil from the bottle over my head. Power shot through my body.

While this was happening, the angel placed a pair of boots with a padding inside them on my feet. I heard the Lord saying, "I have ordained you for ministry." To be ordained by a pastor is one thing, but to be ordained by the Lord Himself is truly something else!

I HAVE GIVEN YOU A HEALING HAND

One night, the Lord appeared to me in my house. He was sitting on a chair and I was on my knees facing Him. He held my hands and started sharing with me about His kingdom. I do not remember everything He told me, but I remember His smile and the love on His face.

About an hour into the conversation, the Lord looked at me and said, "I have given you a healing hand." He went on to say, "You will go to the nations of the world and preach the gospel. You will demonstrate My power with great signs and wonders. When you lift your right hand, My power will flow through it. Use the authority I am giving you." Right after He said that, I got up and walked out the door of my house to preach the gospel. I did not know where I was going. I was just so excited to put it to work.

Then the Lord showed me a vision. I was a minister in a European country and I was having lunch in a restaurant. As I was sitting, I noticed a large poster of a lion by the cashier's stand. Suddenly the lion came alive and began moving and walking. I finished eating and went to pay my bill. The cashier said to me, "The manager wants to see you." As I was wondering why, I heard a commotion and noise outside the restaurant. I looked through the open door and saw a group of people shouting, "He is dead! He is dead!" I ran out of the restaurant and across the street, pushing people aside to get to the dead man. I lifted him up from the pavement and said, "In the name of Jesus, death, give him up!" The man started vomiting. He was raised up from death.

Since that vision, I have laid my hands on many sick people and they have been healed. The blind have received their sight, deaf ears have opened, cancer has disappeared, and demons have been cast out, all in Jesus' name.

Jesus, Peter, John, James, and I

The Spirit of the Lord carried me away again to the place where the Lord first appeared to me in 1972. I saw the Lord Jesus walking with Peter, John, and James. They were coming into a temple where I was standing. This time, Jesus had dark brown hair to His ears and a dark complexion. As He was coming closer to where I was standing, I could see He was smiling. It was a smile of utter love and delight. As I stood there gazing into His eyes, He pointed His finger toward me and simply said, "Bella."

Jesus, Peter, John, and James were conversing with each other as they walked into the upper room where I was standing. As I was wondering why the Lord used this Italian word, *bella*, I realized He knew that I spoke a little Italian. The word is translated "very good" or "beautiful." The Hebrew equivalent of this word is used more than once in the Book of Genesis.

When God created the earth, He was so pleased. Repeatedly in Genesis 1 we read that God "saw that [His Creation] was good." I understood that the Master was pleased with the work He has called me to do. Then I saw Peter, John, and James smile at me as they were entering the temple. What a blessing it is for the Lord to say to you, "Well done, my faithful servant." Jesus was identifying Himself with His servant.

5

ANGELIC VISITATION

But to which of the angels has He ever said: "Sit at My right hand, Till I make Your enemies Your footstool"? Are they not all ministering spirits sent forth to minister for those who will inherit salvation?

—Hebrews 1:13–14

NGELS ANNOUNCED THE birth of Christ and ministered to Him throughout His life on Earth. Throughout the Bible, angels ministered, proclaiming the words of the Lord to mankind.

The angels of the Lord will never reveal anything that is contrary to Scripture. They will never add anything or take anything away from the Word of God. In other words, the angels of the Lord will neither invent an additional Bible nor will they distort Scripture. The Word of God is always the standard.

Once, in a dream, I was walking in a park and I saw a large spaceship flying above me. A few seconds later the same spaceship turned around and landed about 150 feet away from where I was standing. Doors opened all over the ship and creatures I had never seen before in my life stepped out. As they were approaching me I noticed that from the neck down they had human bodies. They were all in military uniform. Each wore a wide belt with a large golden buckle, which had some kind of design on it. Their pants were tucked inside military boots.

As they came closer, fear gripped me, and I heard myself repeatedly saying, "If God is for us, who can be against us?" (Rom 8:31). Suddenly, I saw a great multitude of people standing behind me, repeating what I was saying. I saw the first living creature's face, and it looked like a lion; the second looked like a calf; the third looked like a flying eagle; and the fourth living creature had the face of a man. The fourth living creature—a man who was wearing a bright white robe—stood before me and said, "Do not be afraid. We are here to protect you and to see how you are doing." I noticed that as the man was speaking, the other living creatures were at attention. When I came out of the dream, the Holy Spirit led me to Revelation 4:6–7:

> Before the throne there was a sea of glass, like crystal. And in the midst of the throne, and around the throne, were four living creatures full of eyes in front and in back. The first living creature was like a lion, the second living creature like a calf, the third living creature had a face like a man, and the fourth living creature was like a flying eagle.

Who are these living creatures? We see them in Revelation 4 and in Isaiah 6. Their task is to praise and worship the King of Glory in and around the throne of God. Notice that both the seraphim and the living creatures have wings. They fly around the throne of God and worship Him.

The four living creatures are created only to serve and worship. They also use their wings to cover their eyes from the glory that comes out from the Lord. These high-ranking angels are "full of eyes around and within" (Rev. 4:8), which enable them to see the past, present, and the future. They have been given these eyes so they can see what the Lord has done, what He is doing at the present time, and what He is about to do in the future. They "do not rest day or night, saying: 'Holy, holy, holy, Lord God Almighty, Who was and is and is to come!'" (v. 8).

These creatures are aware of God's creation (the past); they are aware of the Cross and His resurrection (the now); and they are aware of His judgment (the future). Their eyes are not like our eyes; they have the eyes of understanding. When I visited heaven,

I was given "the eyes of....understanding being enlightened" to see the works of His mighty power (Eph. 1:18).

HOST OF ANGELS IN EARTH

I have been ministering to the nations of the world via telephone as an intercessory prayer warrior for many years. In January 2005, the Spirit of the Lord lifted me up and placed me in the prayer room at Trinity Broadcasting Network. Suddenly I saw a screen in front of me. There were circles of ocean waves flowing out from the screen. The waves were followed by a thick white cloud, and heavenly music and worship were coming through the cloud. I saw heaven open. Radiant light, white clouds, music and worship were descending out of heaven. I saw the wave of clouds and the music and worship extend from the screen and fill the prayer room. A host of angels wearing brilliant white robes also filled the room. Some of the angels were flying in the cloud and some were walking in the room.

As I was sitting and observing the activity of heaven and enjoying the heavenly music and the beauty of the angels, I saw a figure emerging from that glorious white cloud. It was the Lord Jesus Christ. He walked through the prayer room touching and blessing each one of the prayer warriors. I heard the prayer warriors saying, "Who touched me?" Then I realized I was the only one in the room who could see the revelation and the manifestation of the activity of heaven.

I noticed a tall man standing in the room. It was Billy Graham. I also noticed that all the angels had wings. The music, the worship and praise, the beauty and the glory of God that was coming out of heaven was breathtaking. I had heard some of the worship music before on previous visits to heaven. The activity in the room was an extension of heaven as it connected with Earth.

My overall feeling was of complete harmony with the perfection and total integration of everything around me. Somehow, I was a part of it; part of the harmony, part of the perfection. I was not just seeing and hearing what was around me; I was integrated into it. I did not just experience joy and love and purity and harmony; I somehow became part of them, and they became part of me. It was like the experiences I had had in heaven all over again. Then I saw the Lord, the cloud, the angels, and the music and worship disappear.

Let me tell you something about this network: it is God's network. I have been with Trinity Broadcasting Network since 2001. The Lord sent me there to minister, and in that prayer room millions have come to know Christ. Thousands have been healed and delivered from sickness. We have received calls from all over the world, twenty-four hours a day, seven days a week, for over thirty-four years. The prayers there never sleep.

TBN is an extension of heaven. That prayer room is holy ground. Many tears have been shed in that room as we minister to hurting people. I myself have received and handled over one hundred thousand calls over the last five years. Trinity Broadcasting Network produces pastors, teachers, prophets, apostles, and evangelists for the fivefold ministries. I am a product of this great "God's network."

There is a mighty, tangible anointing flowing from the holy ground of TBN to the airwaves and into the homes of the nations of the world. TBN is all about souls, for the very heart of the Lord is souls. I am grateful to the Lord Jesus Christ. I am grateful to Trinity Broadcasting Network and to His generals.

The Man Behind This Great Network

I am going to tell you about the man behind God's network, Dr. Paul Crouch. He is a man after God's own heart. For the last five years that I have been with TBN, I have had the opportunity to talk with Dr. Crouch and his wife, Jan, and their son (one of God's young generals), the visionary Paul Jr. I know them to be down-to-earth, tenderhearted people.

Almost daily I would see this prophet of God, Dr. Crouch, when he would come to address the nations of the world or behind the scenes during the *Praise the Lord* broadcasts. Dr. Crouch would give us the thumbs-up and say, "Good job." To my joy, I was blessed to have coffee with Dr. Crouch and get to know the general's heart.

ONE-ON-ONE CONVERSATION

It was August 2, 2007, and we were in the midst of a "Macedonian week," one characterized by generosity. I was assigned to Studio C. There was a temporary coffee/recreation room at this studio, and my job was to entertain the guests who came to help with the praise-a-thon and make sure no one crossed the line where all the cameras were.

Around three o'clock in the afternoon, I was standing facing the prayer room. I heard a voice behind me say, "How are you, sir?" I turned around to see Dr. Paul Crouch.

I said, "Yes, sir. I didn't see you, Dr. Crouch. How are you doing, sir? You look strong and healthy. Good to see you." The general stopped, faced me, and said with a beautiful smile and vibrant look, "Do you know what today is?" He caught me by surprise; I didn't know what he was talking about. I looked at him and said, "Your birthday?" The general replied, "No! Today is TBN's thirty-fourth birthday." I said to him, "Praise the Lord! TBN will be running until Jesus comes." He said "Yes! Yes! We will be praising the Lord until then." He then said, "Let me go greet the prayer partners." Dr. Crouch and I walked through the open glass door. He was waving his thumbs-up and greeting his prayer partners. I have witnessed him do this for over five years; that's just the kind of person he is.

The next day, I was walking around Studio C when the general came in and waved his hand toward me. We greeted each other and he asked me a few questions about the praise-a-thon. Dr. Crouch and I began a one-on-one conversation about the Lord. I pointed my finger toward the prayer room and said, "Dr. Crouch, that prayer room is holy ground. There are many souls that have been saved and many tears that have been shed in that room." The general agreed, "Yes, TBN is reaching the whole world, and we are going to be preaching until Jesus comes." I said, "Dr. Crouch, I saw your grandson, Brandon, in Singapore and Uganda. I saw how the Lord is working on him. I saw the spirit of humbleness in him."

Just then one of the managers of the prayer department came and handed Dr. Crouch a slip of paper. Written on the slip was the praise report of a lady who had accepted Christ and also needed a little prayer. As he was reading the slip of paper, Dr. Crouch said, "Let us hold hands and pray for this dear woman." I took Dr. Crouch's hand and two other women joined us. I tell you the truth, I saw tears in the general's eyes. He has a very sensitive and tender heart for souls.

Dr. Crouch greeted each man and woman that came to help with the praise-a-thon. All I ever saw in him was the love of God. I tell you the truth, during the thirty-minute conversation I had with the general, I felt the same peace, love, joy, and acceptance I had experienced during one my visitations and conversations with the living Christ.

As I neared completing this book, the Holy Spirit spoke to my heart to include a section about that man's heart. I must also say regarding his son, Paul Jr.; his wife, Jan; and the grandchildren, Brittney and Brandon; that I have talked with each of them many times and they all have the heart of the Father.

On one of my many trips to heaven, the Lord showed me His generals, and Paul Crouch is one of them. I am giving honor to whom honor is due. As the anointing was found on Aaron on Mount Hermon—for the Lord has bestowed His blessing, even life forevermore—the anointing on me found me in Trinity Broadcasting Network. (See Psalm 133.) After all, it is all about Jesus. It is about *souls*!

6

THE LORD REJECTED A PASTOR

I know your works, that you are neither cold nor hot. I could wish you were cold or hot. So then, because you are lukewarm, neither cold nor hot, I will vomit you out of My mouth.
—Revelation 3:15–16

RIGHT AFTER THE Lord showed me the vision of the disobedient Christians waiting for the day of judgment, He showed me a vision of a church where I once ministered. It was a denominational church that did not believe the full doctrine of Christ. From the pulpit, the pastor would regularly mock Pentecostal preachers, among other things.

In the first vision I saw the Lord and myself standing at the door of that church. The Lord told me He was grieved with what was going on inside the church. Then He vanished. I walked inside the church and saw people in torment. The floor was filthy and covered with worms. The people were crying for help, but there was no help. It looked like hell.

In the second vision, the Lord and I were standing in an empty warehouse. A man was sitting in the fetal position, clearly in torment. The man was the pastor of that church. I stepped forward to pray for him and the Lord stopped me. He said, "No! He has rejected my Word, so I have rejected him, and the evil spirit is troubling him."

Pastors, love for one another is love for God. Preach the uncompromising Word of God. Remember the Word of God is God Himself. (See John 1:1.) He cannot be altered, added to, or taken away from. We have an obligation and responsibility to give a true report concerning the Lord. The Bible says Jesus "was moved with compassion" (Matt. 9:36; 14:14; Mark 1:41; 6:34). Compassion is love; likewise, "God is love" (1 John 4:8). We must be moved by what God has said, not by our feelings.

Pastors, don't compromise the Word of God. The Word of God is God Himself. Remember, when you read the Word, the Word reads you. Our hearts are so deceitful; who can know a man's heart but God (Jer. 17:9)? You can run, but you cannot hide from Him. The Father is not delighted when we walk according to the flesh. We must be spiritually minded. (See Romans 8:1–8.)

Pastors, don't bring strife to your church. When you are not walking in love and you have strife in your life, the gifts of the Holy Spirit stop. (See 1 Corinthians 13:1–13.) Stand on the Word of God and take control of your feelings. Strife is born out of our emotions. To control your emotions, you must control your tongue. The Bible says that the person who can control his words can gain mastery over his entire body (James 3:2).

Speak the Word to your congregation. Some will hear you and some will not. Regardless, do not compromise the true Word of God. Be a dedicated pleaser of God; make the quality no-turning-back decision. If you do not understand the Word itself, you will not understand how it works. Be filled with the Holy Ghost. Demonstrate the Word with signs and wonders. It is all about Jesus; it is all about souls. Step back from the pulpit and let the Holy Spirit step in. A church that does not win souls is a dead church. If you cannot demonstrate the gospel, you are not fit to preach the gospel. Jesus said it. I did not. (See Mark 16:15–18.)

If your church refuses to preach the full gospel, leave and find a good Bible-teaching church. "Let the dead bury their own dead" (Matt. 8:22).

Pastors, you must practice what you preach. Your faith and confidence must rest on the infallible Word of God, not on your own shrewd dealings. A person who is anointed by the call of God speaks the Word of the Lord in the name of the Lord. They carry weight in the church by virtue of the ethical, moral, and spiritual urgency of their message. Their credentials, credibility, and status do not truly come by official designation, but by the power of their inner calling and by the response of those who hear them. So be a God-pleaser rather than a man-pleaser. Do not be like the disobedient Christians the Lord once showed me, who were waiting for Judgment Day.

> Then He said to the disciples, "It is impossible that no offenses should come, but woe to him through whom they do come! It would be better for him if a millstone were hung around his neck, and he were thrown into the sea, than that he should offend one of these little ones."
> —Luke 17:1–2

THE WORD WORKS IF YOU WORK IT

So I sought for a man among them who would make a wall, and stand in a gap before Me on behalf of the land, that I should not destroy it; but I found no one.
—**Ezekiel 22:30**

RE YOU INTERCEDING for your land, for your government, for your family, your children, and your children's children? Standing in prayer between God almighty and His children is one thing the devil does not want you doing. There is power in prayer, wonder-working power. Miracles happen when we pray. Souls are transformed when we pray. Lives are changed when we pray. Demons tremble when we pray. Sickness disappears when we pray. Satan is defeated when we pray. The dead are resurrected when we pray. We come under a mighty anointing when we pray. God, give us a supernatural desire to pray. The Word of God tells us to pray in the spirit, even when we do not know for what to pray. Let us read Romans 8:26:

> For we do not know what we should pray for as we ought, but the Spirit Himself makes intercession for us with groanings which cannot be uttered.

One of the eleven times the Lord appeared to me, He instructed me to pray in tongues. Since then it has been a revelation, a mystery unfolding. Your heart will be open and the Lord will reveal it to you, Spirit to spirit. Your soul is going to know it. Your body is going to know it. You will be forever transformed. You will never be the same again. You will walk in the spirit realm. You will be possessed by the Holy Spirit.

Stir up the gift within you. You can be connected to the heavenly realm. As Christians, we are not into the natural; we are into the supernatural. The supernatural never bows to the natural. We are not normal. We are abnormal. The people and angels I saw in heaven constantly praise and worship the Lord. When people are not praying here on Earth, the opposite is true. Demons are loosed and souls are lost for eternity when we do not pray. We fall under demonic attack when we do not pray. More prayer, more power. Much prayer, much power. Less prayer, less power. No prayer, no power. "Pray without ceasing" (1 Thess. 5:17).

Prayer is the foundation for success in every Christian endeavor. Jesus is your example. Have you ever noticed how often the Bible mentions that Jesus withdrew to a lonely place to pray?

> And in the morning, rising up a great while before day, he went out, and departed into a solitary place, and there prayed.
>
> —Mark 1:35, KJV

> And it came to pass in those days, that he went out into a mountain to pray, and continued all night in prayer to God.
>
> —Luke 6:12, KJV

These are just two of many instances recorded in the Gospels.

Jesus was in continual communication with God through prayer. He spent hours every day separated from the people, fellowshiping with His heavenly Father. If Jesus had a need for preparation through prayer, how much more should we?

The Anointing

Many scriptures throughout the Bible speak of the anointing. Psalm 92:10 says, "But my horn You have exalted like a wild ox; I have been anointed with fresh oil." Fresh anointing oil is what we need if we are going to be able to fulfill that which the Lord has already spoken clearly.

Isaiah speaks of the power of anointing to break the yoke of bondage, evil, and oppression. The anointing also carries the power to do good and bring healing.

> God anointed Jesus of Nazareth with the Holy Spirit and with power; how he went about doing good and healing all who were oppressed by the devil, for God was with Him.
>
> —Acts 10:38, NRSV

The anointing is the manifestation of the Holy Spirit operating upon or through an individual or a corporate group to produce the work of Jesus. It is God in you and God with you and God around you. When you are under the anointing of the Holy Spirit, you are walking in His shadow. When you are under the anointing, miracles happen, souls are transformed, and demons are troubled. Give thanks for the anointing.

When I am under a mighty anointing, I am not the same. The Holy Spirit takes over; great power flows from inside me that I cannot control. My body jerks. The word of knowledge, the word of wisdom, the gifs of healing operate better. I can discern spirits much better. My faith reaches an all-time high. On the other hand, the anointing that I carry draws all kinds of demons from every-where to me, even from Christians. I experience persecution, and you will, too. But be cheerful, for the Lord has overcome it.

The anointing is very precious and must be protected. Do not lose it. If you think you need more of the anointing, ask the Holy Spirit to reveal Jesus to you. I tell you the truth, you will be moving tremendously in this manner. Ask the Holy Spirit to possess you. He will.

Interpreting Dreams

Generally speaking, the Holy Spirit uses different avenues of visionary revelation to speak into our lives, including dreams, visions, and other avenues. Dreams are closely associated with visions. The primary difference is that dreams occur during the hour of sleep, while visions usually take place while one is fully awake or conscious. Both means of visual revelation have solid biblical precedent. The Bible says:

> If there is a prophet among you, I, the LORD, make Myself known to him in a vision; I speak to him in a dream.
>
> —Numbers 12:6

Dreams are the language of emotion and often contain much symbolism. When we interpret dreams we must learn to take our interpretation first from Scripture and then from our own lives. The Bible is full of symbolic images and elements.

God's symbolic language is consistent throughout the Bible. How He speaks in Genesis is similar to how He speaks in Revelation. God is the same yesterday, today, and forevermore. He keeps His Word above His name. Consistency in God's symbolism carries over into our lives as well. In our dreams there may be symbolic actions, symbolic colors, symbolic creatures, symbolic names, symbolic numbers, and symbolic objects.

Numbers are highly symbolic in the Bible, as well as in prophetic dreams. As such, we have to be careful when interpreting the meaning of numbers in dreams. For example, the number three may be interpreted as divine; as representing the Father, the Son, and the Holy Spirit; the resurrection on the third day; or perhaps the outer court, the inner court, and the holy of holies. The number two may be symbolic of agreement (Matt. 18:19), it may represent the two witnesses discussed in the Book of Revelation, or Jesus sending the Seventy two-by-two.

Colors in dreams may be symbolic as well. White may represent purity and light. Red could symbolize bloodshed or the red horse of Revelation 6:4. Amber often symbolizes the glory of God. These few examples are given simply to help you gain insight.

When you dream, remember the symbolic objects, numbers, colors, and creatures in the dream. If you are the focus or "main character" in the dream, it may very well be about you. If you are a participant in the dream, generally the message is about someone to whom you are connected, like a family member or someone from your church. If you are outside the action in the dream, observing, then it is about someone to whom you are not connected. God speaks in dreams to warn us, encourage us, or to direct us toward our future.

Dreams can be exciting and wonderful as a means of receiving insight and revelation, as long as they come from the right source. Remember that dreams can arise from three places: the demonic realm, the soul realm (our own human mind and spirit), and the Holy Spirit. In order to be effective, we must be able to distinguish the source of the dream. Ask the Lord to give you the gift of discernment. Be a student of the Bible. Have the mind of Christ and a receptive heart.

BIBLICAL EXAMPLES OF DREAMS

- Abimelech (Gen. 20:3–7)
- Laban (Gen. 31:24)
- A Midianite soldier (Judg.7:13–15)
- Pharaoh's butler and baker (Gen. 40:1–23)
- Pharaoh (Gen. 41)
- Nebuchadnezzar (Dan. 2:1–49)
- The wise men (Matt. 2:12)
- Pilate's wife (Matt. 27:19)
- Joseph (Gen. 35:7–11)

Biblical Symbols

Symbolic colors

- Amber—The glory or presence of God
- Black—Sin, death, or a stranger
- Blue—Heaven or Holy Spirit
- Scarlet—Blood atonement, sacrifice
- Purple—Kingship, royalty
- Red—Bloodshed, war
- White—Purity, light, righteousness
- Green—Life, intercession

Symbolic numbers

- One—God, beginning, source
- Two—Witnesses, testimony
- Three—Godhead, divine, completeness
- Four—Earth, creation, winds, seasons
- Five—Cross, grace
- Six—Man, beast, Satan
- Seven—Perfection, completeness
- Eight—New beginning
- Nine—Finality, fullness
- Ten—Law, government
- Eleven—Disorganization, lawlessness
- Twelve—Divine, government, apostolic fullness
- Thirteen—Rebellion, backsliding, apostasy

Work of the Holy Spirit

Many times we wait for the Holy Spirit to move, and we may begin to wonder why He is not moving. But we must realize that the Holy Spirit is always moving. Should we wait for the gifts of the Holy Spirit to move? No! They are already in operation. The problem is that we have not moved into the realm where they are. When you get into the spirit, signs and wonders will follow.

These special gifts—the wonderful visitations, the prophetic visions, the trips to heaven, and all the supernatural events—are the manifestations of the Holy Spirit. Seek Him, and you will find Him (2 Chron. 15:2). Brothers and sisters, the Holy Spirit is working. You are only an instrument, a voice, or a temple. The Holy Spirit fills the temple, He dwells inside, He does the work. You are only a voice; He reveals.

The same Jesus has come for one purpose: that He might be so manifested in us that the world shall see Him. We must be shining lights to reflect such a Holy Jesus. What an inward burning it is to taste of the heaven I have seen and experienced. Thank Him, love Him for each revelation, meditate on it, and apply it specifically to you and your life. Commit yourself to do it and live by it.

What do you hear? Does anyone hear the knock? Jesus is saying, "Behold, I stand at the door and knock" (Rev. 3:20). He is knocking at your door—the door of your heart. Do you answer Him by saying, "Go on somewhere else," and miss the day of your revelation? Or will you open the door and say, "Oh, Jesus, do not pass me by"?

What will you do? Will you ignore the knock until He goes away? Or will you open the door and say, like Joshua, "As for me and my house, we will serve the Lord" (Josh. 24:15)? How will you respond to the Man who is knocking at your door, longing to reveal to you the mysteries and revelations of heaven? Is there anyone? Are there any gatekeepers who will let Him in? Do you hear what I hear?

> And behold, I am coming quickly, and My reward is with Me, to give to every one according to his work. I am the Alpha and the Omega, the Beginning and the End, the First and the Last.
>
> —Revelation 22:12–13

Spiritual Gifts

In 1 Corinthians 12:1 we read: "Now concerning spiritual gifts, brethren, I do not want you to be ignorant." There is a great weakness in the church of Christ because of an awful ignorance concerning the Spirit of God and the gifts He has come to bring. God would have us know His will concerning the power and manifestation of His Spirit. He would have us ever hungry to receive more and more of His Spirit.

It is impossible to overestimate the importance of being filled with the Spirit. It is impossible for us to meet the conditions of the day; to walk in the light, as He is in the light; to subdue kingdoms, work righteousness, and bind the works of Satan unless we are filled with the Holy Spirit. As we look to God, His mind will be made known, and His revelation and His word of wisdom will be forthcoming.

The Word of Knowledge

> To another the word of knowledge by the same Spirit; to another faith by the same Spirit.
> —1 Corinthians 12:8–9

I believe that Satan has many devices, and that they are worse today than ever before. But I also believe that there is to be a full manifestation on the earth of the power and glory of God to defeat every device of Satan. How important it is that we shall have the manifestation of the the word of knowledge in our midst. The Spirit who brings forth the word of wisdom brings forth the word of knowledge. The revelation of the mysteries of God come by the Spirit, and we must have a supernatural word of knowledge in order to convey to others the things that the Spirit of God has revealed. The Spirit of God reveals Christ in all His wonderful fullness, and He shows Him to us from the beginning to the end of the Scriptures. The Scriptures make us wise unto salvation; they open to us the depths of the kingdom of heaven, which reveal all the divine Mind to us.

GIFT OF HEALING

If ye abide in me, and my words abide in you, ye shall ask
what ye will, and it shall be done unto you.

—John 15:7, KJV

The Lord has told us to covet earnestly the best gifts, and we need
to be covetous for those that will bring Him the most glory. People
need to see the gifts of healing and the working of miracles in
operation today. The man who is going through with God, to be
used in healing, must be a man of longsuffering. He must be always
ready with a word of comfort. If the sick one is in distress and
helpless and does not see everything eye to eye with you, you must
bear with him. Our Lord Jesus Christ was filled with compassion
and lived and moved in a place of longsuffering. We will have to
get into that same place if we are to help those in need.

Sometimes when I pray for the sick, I am apparently rough. But
I am not dealing with the person, I am dealing with the satanic
forces that are binding that person. In healing, your heart is full of
love and compassion for all, but you are moved to a holy anger as
you see the place the devil has taken in the body of the sick one. I
tend to deal with Satan's position with real forcefulness.

Smith Wigglesworth, a great apostle of the faith of the late
1800s and early 1900s, told this story: "One day a pet dog followed
a lady out of her house and ran all around her feet. She said to the
dog, 'My dear, I cannot have you with me today.' The dog wagged
its tail and made a big fuss. She said, 'Go home, my dear.' But the
dog did not go. At last she shouted roughly, 'Go home!' and off
it went."[1]

Some people deal with the devil like that. The devil can stand
all the comfort you'd like to give him. Cast him out! You are not
dealing not with the person; you are dealing with the devil. When
you deal with a sickness like cancer, recognize that it is a living
evil spirit that is destroying the body.

I prayed for a man once who was suffering from lung cancer.
He could not talk because the cancer had not only eaten his lungs

but also his vocal chords. Before I prayed for him, the Spirit of the Lord revealed to me that the sickness was demonic. As I started to command the demon of cancer, the demons started to manifest. They all came out, one by one. The man was freed and his voice returned. I'll tell you what, I believe every sickness is instigated by the devil. God does not put sickness on His children. God is a good God. In this particular case, the demons had destroyed the man's body.

Remember, it is Jesus who heals, not you. If the person does not receive his or her healing, do not ask why. Just pray. The reason is a secret between the Lord and the person. There are things that are revealed to us, and there are also things that are not revealed to us. Deuteronomy 29:29 tells us: "The secret things belong to the Lord our God, but those things which are revealed belong to us and to our children forever, that we may do all the words of this law." If God wants us to know, He would have told us. You keep on preaching faith and healing just like you've been preaching it. Remember, God is a good God. He wants every one of His children to be healed.

Imitate Me, Just as I Imitate Christ

The following testimony from Smith Wigglesworth, who once said, "Imitate me, just as I imitate Christ," will build your faith.[2]

❧An Urgent Telegram❧

During the early years of his ministry, Wigglesworth received a desperate telegram from a town some two hundred miles away. They were pleading with him to come pray for a young woman. Without hesitation, Smith traveled the distance as quickly as possible.

Upon his arrival, Wigglesworth discovered that a young woman had become a raging demonic. Her parents and husband were distraught over the situation. They could not even bring her baby to her to nurse, for fear of the harm she might do to herself or the infant.

The family led Wigglesworth up a staircase to a room where the young mother was on the floor, being held down by five men. Even though she physically looked very frail, the evil power controlling her was more than a match for the five men.

As Wigglesworth entered the room, the evil spirit that possessed her stared out of her eyes and snarled at him, "We are many. You cannot cast us out." With complete calm, Wigglesworth firmly stated, "Jesus can. Greater is He that is in me than he that is in the world."

"She is ours. We will not give her up!" The demonic voices growled repeatedly, filling the house with hideous laughter.

Undaunted, Wigglesworth commanded, "Be quiet. In the name of Jesus, come out of her, you foul spirits!"

With a shriek and one last attempt to retain their grasp on the woman, thirty-seven different demonic spirits came out of her, giving their names as they exited. At the authority of the name of Jesus, demons had to relinquish their territory, and the woman was totally delivered.

GIFT OF PROPHECY

In 1 Corinthians 12:10, speaking of the diversities of gifts by the same Spirit, Paul writes: "To another prophecy." We find the importance of the gift of prophecy in 1 Corinthians 14:1, where we are told to follow after charity and desire spiritual gifts, but rather that we may prophesy. We also find that "he who prophesies speaks edification and exhortation and comfort to men" (v. 3).

How important it is, then, that this gift be manifested in the church, in order that the saints might be built up, made strong, and receive the comfort of God. By means of prophecy we receive that which is the mind of the Lord. A prophet is a voice of God. What the prophet hears is spoken by God. We read in the Book of Revelation that "the testimony of Jesus is the spirit of prophecy"

(Rev. 19:10). You will find that true prophetic utterance always exalts the Lamb of God.

No prophetic touch is of any good unless there is holy fire in it. I never expect to be used of God till the fire burns. I feel that if I ever speak it must be by the Spirit at the same time. Remember, the prophet must prophesy according to his or her measure of faith. If you rise up in your weakness, but rise up in love because you want to honor God and just begin, you will find the presence of the Lord upon you. Act in faith and the Lord will meet you. May God take us on and on into this glorious fact of faith, that we may be so directed by the Holy Spirit that God will work through us the miraculous and the prophetic. May we always know that it is no longer we but He who is working through us to bring forth His own divine, good pleasure.

THE DISCERNING OF SPIRITS

Discerning of spirits is the supernatural ability to recognize and distinguish between not only good and bad spirits, but various classes of spirits.

- the Holy Spirit
- good angels
- fallen angels
- demons or evil spirits
- the human spirits

Discerning is a form of direct perception where knowledge is the impartation of fact. Discernment is perception, a feeling, a sight-oriented ability; whereas a word of knowledge is a fact that is dropped into our thoughts or spirit.

Discerning of spirits is the supernatural capacity to judge whether the spirit operating has a source that is human, demonic, or divine. It is supernatural perception in the spiritual realm for the purpose of determining the source of spiritual activity. The discerning of spirits gives insight into the spiritual world. It is supernatural insight into the realm of spirits. To discern means to see, whether it be divine spirits, evil spirits, the human spirit, or even the discerning of the similitude of God. Spiritual discernment is the grace to see into the unseen. It is a gift of the Spirit to perceive what is in the spirit. Its purpose is to see into the nature of that which is veiled.

How to Hear His Voice

My sheep hear My voice, and I know them, and they follow Me.

—John 10:27

The Lord speaks to us through many different avenues, including visions, dreams, and angelic visitation. Another means of communication with the Holy Spirit is by "inner knowing." We simply know that we know that we know. He also speaks to us through His inner voice. Yet our most important source of revelation is the Word (the Scripture).

Since the Bible is our absolute, infallible, unchanging standard of truth, we must test all spiritual experience. The Bible tells us to "test the spirits" (1 John 4:1). The Scriptures tell us that spiritual revelation comes from any of three sources: the Holy Spirit, the human soul, and the realm of evil spirits. But the Holy Spirit is the only source of true revelation. It was the Holy Spirit who "moved" the prophets of the Old Testament (2 Pet. 1:21). "The Spirit Himself bears witness with our spirit that we are children of God" (Rom. 8:16). The Holy Spirit within the believer always confirms true revelation from the Holy Spirit. The Holy Spirit is "the Spirit of truth" (John 16:13). He rejects that which is false.

Still Small Voice

In 1 Kings 19, we see how the Lord manifest to the prophet of Elijah while he was running for his life from the wicked Queen Jezebel. Elijah was hiding in a cave, and during the night the word of the Lord came to him. He said to Elijah, "What are you doing here, Elijah?" (v. 9). The Lord said:

> "Go out, and stand on the mountain before the LORD." And behold, the LORD passed by, and a great and strong wind tore into the mountains and broke the rocks in pieces before the LORD, but the LORD was not in the wind; and after the wind an earthquake, but the LORD was not in the earthquake; and after the earthquake a fire, but the LORD was not in the fire; and after the fire a still small voice.
>
> —1 Kings 19:11–12

We are surrounded by so much noise we often miss God's voice.

Now let me tell you a story I heard: There was a man named Mr. Henry. Mr. Henry thought he had a hearing problem and decided to see his doctor. When he got there he told the doctor, "I think I have a hearing problem, could you check me?" The doctor took his wristwatch and placed it against his ear to see if he could hear the ticking of the watch. Mr. Henry paused for a second and then he said, "Yes." The doctor stepped back about ten feet and said, "Mr. Henry, can you hear me?" Mr. Henry paused for a second again and said, "Yes, I can hear you." The doctor went to another room and said, "Mr. Henry, can you hear me?" Mr. Henry paused for a second and then said, "Yes, I can hear you." Then the doctor came back to the room and said, "Mr. Henry, you don't have a hearing problem, you have a listening problem."

God is always speaking, but are you listening? How do I know that the voice I am hearing is God? Well, it will edify you, exhort you, and comfort you. But the devil's most common attacks are condemnation and discouragement.

God is peace. If the voice does not give you peace, reject it. The Bible says, "My sheep hear my voice, and I know them, and they know me" (John 10:27). Knowing God is to know the voice of God.

The Holy Spirit has His own distinctive character. He is not aggressive or pushy, nor does He shout at us. He usually speaks in soft tones and directs us by gentle impulses. To receive His direction we must be attentive to His voice and sensitive to His impulses. The Holy Spirit deals with us as individuals. The Holy Spirit respects our uniqueness. No one is a carbon copy of another. We are all original. We have to depend on the Holy Spirit for guidance. It is the only pathway to spiritual maturity. Ask the Holy Spirit to open your heart and your mind. He will.

THE POWER OF THE TONGUE

> Death and life are in the power of the tongue. And those
> who love it will eat its fruit.
>
> —Proverbs 18:21

Brothers and sisters, watch your mouth and guard your tongue. The Bible tells us there is power in the tongue when we speak. If you speak against blessing, you will be cursed. If you speak against healing, your second home just may the hospital. If you speak against prosperity, you will be broke, busted, and disgusted all the days of your life.

The Book of James tells us a double-minded man is unstable in all his ways (James 1:8). Think before you speak. Do not run your mouth. For a man who cannot control his tongue, his whole belief in Christ is in vain; all is vanity. The earth was formed by the spoken word. Speak blessings over your life, over your children, and your children's children. Let the Word sink into your heart, for as a man "thinks in his heart, so is he" (Prov. 23:7). Whatever you say, you shall have it.

LISTEN, WATCH, WAIT

> Now therefore, listen to me, my children, For blessed are
> those who keep my ways. Hear instruction and be wise,
> And do not disdain it. Blessed is the man who listens to

me, Watching daily at my gates, Waiting at the posts of
my doors. For whoever finds me finds life, And obtains
favor from the LORD; But he who sins against me wrongs
his own soul; All those who hate me love death.

—Proverbs 8:32–36

There are three principles to hearing the voice of the Lord. One
must listen, and upon listening watch and keep on watching, and
then wait and keep on waiting. In order to listen we have to shut
our mouth. We cannot speak and hear at the same time. Watching
at the gates means staying alert; expectation leads to revelation.
Waiting at the door means standing by to hear what the Lord will
speak. Remember, the voice of the Lord usually does not come
from outside of us. Sometimes the Lord will speak to us audibly,
but most of the time His voice is heard inside of us, in our hearts.
Be still in reverence and worship, and listen.

The inner life prepares us for the outer life. We must maintain
our inner life to be effective in our outer life. We must mature
and maintain our inner communion and fellowship with God. We
must pay attention to our heart, for that is where God dwells. God
is speaking. Are you listening? "My sheep hear my voice, and I
know them, and they know me" (John 10:27). Each time we hear
the voice of the Lord and obey Him, we are further anointed,
empowered, consumed, and possessed by the Spirit of God. We
must learn to respond every time He calls. Remain sensitive to
His call, and you will grow. He wants to speak into every area of
your life. He wants to share your joys and your hardships, for He
is your Father. At every call you are becoming more completely
clothed with the Spirit of His Son. Thank Him for each revelation.
Meditate on it. Apply it specifically to you and your life. Commit
yourself to do and live by it. Do not rush ahead in the pursuit of
intellectual knowledge, but allow the Holy Spirit to build faith
and expectation in you "precept upon precept, line upon line"
(Isa. 28:13).

Be a flame of fire; a man burning with the Spirit of God. Burn
with passion to know God and to commune with Him. Burn with

passion for God's Word, for souls, for Holy Ghost manifestation, for holiness, and for Christlikeness. Hunger after God and never be satisfied with your present position. Press on to the fullness of the Spirit.

POWER OF FASTING

> But you, when you fast, anoint your head and wash your face, so that you do not appear to men that you are fasting, but to your Father who is in the secret place; and your Father who sees in secret will reward you openly.
> —Matthew 6:17–18

The great apostle of faith Smith Wigglesworth once said, "Anyone can be ordinary, but it takes someone of great faith to be extraordinary."[3] Remember, we serve an extraordinary God. Brothers and sisters, when you fast you are crucifying yourself with Christ. Your flesh becomes dead while your spirit becomes alive in Him. Your mind becomes the mind of Christ; you talk like Jesus, you walk like Jesus, you live like Jesus, and you love like Jesus.

The devil knows that if he can capture your thoughts, he has won a mighty victory. Do not give the devil a place in your mind (Eph. 4:27). If the devil reminds you of your past, which is under the blood, remind him of his future in the pit of hell. If you want the power of God in your life, never look back. Always move forward. The present and future will keep you alive. If you practice this, your future will look much better than your present.

If you are filled with the Holy Spirit, you must never say, "I cannot." You are not normal. The Christian life is not normal. It is supernatural. Fasting gives you boldness. When fear is removed from your life, power and confidence will fill the void and you will begin to walk in the right way, which is God's way.

Remember, the purpose of fasting is not to influence God into acting on your behalf. Abstaining from food does not impress Him. The true purpose of fasting is to shut off the influence of our flesh so we may be in tune with the Spirit. Fasting helps us to receive from

God, but it does not push God into action. Fasting is a tool we use that puts us in a position to be more spiritually aware and "tuned in" to God, so that we can better receive or hear from Him.

When you fast you have a reward coming. The reward is whatever motivated you to fast. Whatever your motive is, establish it by faith and proclaim it before you enter the fast. Expect to receive it. God will see in secret and you will receive openly.

What is the fast God has chosen? Isaiah 58 deals with fasting and observance of the Lord's ordinance. In this chapter the Lord says:

> Is this not the fast I have chosen: To loose the bonds of wickedness, To undo the heavy burdens, To let the oppressed go free, And that you break every yoke? Is it not to share your bread with the hungry, And that you bring to your house the poor who are cast out?
>
> —Isaiah 58:6–7

Brothers and sisters, when I go into a fast, things start happening. I begin to see angels and I have visitations from the Lord. My mind is keen, I have boldness, my eyes are sharp to the spirit realm, and miracles start happening. I see, with the eyes of a seer, visions and dreams. Always go for greater glory from one height of faith to the next height of faith. Do not park in your failure. Just move forward. Paul tells us in Philippians 3:12–13:

> Not that I have already attained, or am already perfected; but I press on, that I may lay hold of that for which Christ Jesus has also laid hold of me. Brethren, I do not count myself to have apprehended; but one thing I do, forgetting those things which are behind and reaching forward to those things which are ahead.

KEEP YOUR EYES ON JESUS

Jesus is "the author and finisher of our faith" (Heb. 12:2). Develop an intimate relationship with Him. Keep your vision alive; it will direct you into your future. Keep your vision for yourself; do not share it with anyone. People will kill your vision. Every promise He has given to you will come to pass. Hold on to your vision.

> For the vision is yet for an appointed time; But at the end it will speak, and it will not lie. Though it tarries, wait for it; Because it will surely come, It will not tarry.
> —Habakkuk 2:3

Do not let the devil sidetrack your vision. Keep your eyes on the road to your destiny. Know that there are many exits along your way. They may appear to be good exits, but know they are not the right exits for you. God will give you a vision, but He will not show you how to get there. The *how* is not revealed. There will be hills, valleys, mountains, and dark tunnels to go through. But there is always a way out. Follow the narrow road to Calvary, which is marked by bloodshed. Do not be moved by what you see. Everything is subject to change. Keep your eyes on Jesus.

> Enter by the narrow gate; for wide is the gate and broad is the way that leads to destruction, and there are many who go in by it.
> —Matthew 7:13

WHO AM I IN CHRIST JESUS?

I am a joint-heir with Christ.
I am the temple of God.
I am a member of Christ's body.
I am a new creation.
I am a prisoner of Christ.
I am a citizen of heaven.

I am an alien and stranger to this world.
I am an enemy of the devil.
I am born of God.
I am the salt of the world.
I am the light of the world.
I am a friend of Christ.
I am a slave to righteousness.
I am the fullness of God.
I am the expression of God.
I am the image of God.
I am the imitator of God.
I am the voice of God.
I am the child of God.
I am an ambassador of God.
I am the speaking spirit.
I am what He said I am.
I have what He said I would have.
I can do what He said I can do.

WHO IS THIS KING OF GLORY?

He is my Savior; He is my Comforter; He is my Healer.
He is my Baptizer of the Holy Spirit.
He is Elohim (the Creator).
He is El Elyon (the God Most High).
He is El Roi (the God Who sees).
He is El Shaddai (the All-sufficient One).
He is Adonai (the Lord).
He is Jehovah-jireh (the Lord Will Provide).
He is Jehovah-rapha (the Lord Who Heals).
He is Jehovah-nissi (the Lord My Banner).
He is Jehovah-shalom (the Lord Is Peace).
He is the Lilly of the Valley and bright Morning Star.
He is the Rose of Sharon.

He is a consuming fire.
He is the Sound of many waters and mighty thunder.
He is the Lion of Judah.
He is the King of kings and the Lord of lords.
He is Jesus Christ of Nazareth, the Son of the Living
God, my friend and your friend.

This Book of the Law shall not depart from your mouth,
but you shall meditate in it day and night, that you may
observe to do according to all that is written in it. For
then you will make your way prosperous, and then you
will have good success.

—Joshua 1:8

8

SPIRITUAL WARFARE

Nor give place to the devil.

—Ephesians 4:27

REMEMBER, THE DEVIL is a thousand times stronger than you. The devil is mighty, but God is almighty. The devil will come to you *like* a roaring lion, but he is not a lion. He is an imposter.

There is power in the blood, wonder-working power. Cover yourself with the blood. Since we have the anointing of God upon us, we pose a serious threat to Satan. In his eyes, we have become the most dangerous living thing on this earth. It is our responsibility to contend with him. Since we represent God's divine power and authority in this world, the adversary must recon with us. When we strap on the full armor of God, we must be prepared and determined to use it. The evil one will certainly attack us with all the forces of darkness. At the same time, be prepared for victory. All the combined forces of hell are not powerful enough to defeat us, for "greater is He that is in you, than he that is in the world" (1 John 4:4, KJV). Glory to God!

The armor of the devil and of his cohorts is restricted to that which is common to man. He is limited; we are not. Remember, the enemy's main tool is fear. Meditate on God's Word. "There is no fear in love; but perfect love casts out fear, because fear involves torment (1 John 4:18). Keep your eyes on Jesus and renew your mind, your heart, and your spirit every day. Be rooted and grounded in the Word of God. Speak the Word "for it is not you who speak, but the Spirit of your Father who speaks in you" (Matt. 10:20).

Once I read a book by a prophet of God who I respect. He said, "Do not go to an enemy's territory and engage in spiritual warfare. We should not invade his territories or he will attack us." Well, brother, my Bible tells me "He who is in [me] is greater than he who is in the world" (1 John 4:4). God has given us authority over the enemy, and there is no reason to be afraid. Fear is the opposite of faith.

The devil has no right to invade our territories. My Bible tells me that "the earth is the LORD's, and the fulness thereof" (Ps. 24:1, KJV). We have dominion and authority over Satan on Earth. The earth is our territory. It has been given to us, and we have the authority to drive out all the forces of darkness. The devil's territories are in the second heaven, not on Earth. The devil is no match for all the power in heaven that is in us.

> When the enemy comes in like a flood, The Spirit of the Lord will lift up a standard against him.
>
> —Isaiah 59:19

Wherever you find the devil, cast him out in the name of Jesus. The demons tremble at the sound of His name. This war is not defensive, it is offensive. We have to go after Satan and destroy his work, in Jesus' name.

WRESTLING WITH THE DEVIL

> Finally, my brethren, be strong in the Lord and in the power of His might. Put on the whole armor of God, that you may be able to stand against the wiles of the devil. For we do not wrestle against flesh and blood, but against principalities, against powers, against the rulers of the darkness of this age, against spiritual hosts of wickedness in the heavenly places. Therefore take up the whole armor of God, that you may be able to withstand in the

evil day, and having done all, to stand. Stand therefore, having girded your waist with truth, having put on the breastplate of righteousness, and having shod your feet with the preparation of the gospel of peace; above all, taking the shield of faith with which you will be able to quench all the fiery darts of the wicked one. And take the helmet of salvation, and the sword of the Spirit, which is the word of God; praying always with all prayer and supplication in the Spirit, being watchful to this end with all perseverance and supplication for all the saints—and for me.

—Ephesians 6:10–19

Since I was called into ministry I have had many encounters with Satan himself. He comes when I am asleep, and sometimes when I am awake! The first time I saw the devil was when he appeared on the wall of my bathroom. I saw a dark image, like a shadow, and I knew it was him. I pointed my finger at him and rebuked him in Jesus' name. That was all it took, one anointed finger!

The next fight I had with Satan was the longest fight I have ever had with him in my ministry. It happened while I was taking a little nap on my couch. I felt a hand grab my neck and a heaviness come over my body. I tried to get up, but I was pressed harder into the couch. The weight was heavy to the point that I could not breathe. Finally, I managed to raise my arm and push him off of me. It felt as if I was pushing a resistant force of wind. I could see his dark body. At first it seemed he was winning the fight. I tried to call upon the name of Jesus, but my tongue would not move, like it was frozen. I felt helpless. Then I heard the still small voice saying, "Why don't you call my name in your heart?" When I said "Jesus" in my heart I saw the devil vanish. Through that fight the Lord taught me that heart-to-heart communication is more effective than verbal.

I Will Kill You

It was about two o'clock in the morning, and I had just finished praying. I took Holy Communion and anointed my head with oil (as I always do before my bedtime). I then heard the voice of the devil very clearly saying, "Tomorrow by this time I will kill you." I said, "Devil, let me get this straight. I don't like you, and you don't like me. Devil, you know who I am. I am A. D. Berhane, the servant of the most high God. You know God has given me authority over you. Now you get behind me, Satan, in Jesus' name!" He left.

The next day I had just finished ministering at Trinity Broadcasting Network. I was heading home around 9:30 p.m. on the Golden State freeway in Los Angeles, California. While I was driving I received a call on my cell phone from a sister in Christ who urgently needed prayer. As I was praying, binding and loosing the devil, I noticed a large piece of concrete that was left in the middle of the freeway. By the time I saw it, it was too late for me to avoid hitting it. I drove right over it, damaging the front of my car and the radiator. Thankfully, I was OK. Then I remembered the threat I received from the devil the night before: "I will kill you." Brothers and sisters, you do not challenge the devil, unless you understand who you are in Christ and the authority given to you. Remember the anointing in you will draw all the darkness in heavenly places.

Sexual Encounter with the Devil

When I was fourteen years of age, a female demon would come to my room on a regular basis. She would come to me by night, while I was asleep. Every time she was in my room, I would sense her presence. With fear all over me I would open my eyes and see her standing on top of my bed, naked. She looked like a mannequin that you see in department stores. She was slim, about five feet tall, and her skin was smooth, silver in color, and oily. Her eyes were slanted and a little different from human eyes. She had very long legs and she was completely bald.

As she stood over my bed she would stare at me. Her presence would grip me with fear, and, without going into details, I would be under her total control. After her regular visitation she would leave the room. She stopped coming only after I was born again. The reason I am sharing this is because of similar experiences I have heard others tell about regarding their encounters with the devil—even Christians.

Genesis 6:1–3 talks about the wickedness and the judgment of man. The human race was rapidly degenerating, despite a few godly men, such as Enosh, Enoch, and Noah. These passages tell of angels who rebelliously left heaven to take women as wives. These sons of God and their human wives produced children who were giants and were later wiped out by the flood.

You might ask how it is possible for a spirit to have a sexual encounter with a human. Well, demons can manifest in human flesh, as Jesus the Spirit manifest to Thomas after the resurrection. The Bible tells us:

> Jesus came, the doors being shut, and stood in the midst, and said, "Peace to you!" Then He said to Thomas, "Reach your finger here, and look at My hands; and reach your hand here, and put it into My side. Do not be unbelieving, but believing."
>
> —John 20:26–27

The Spirit of Jesus put on flesh and bones.

We read also of angels in human form appearing in Sodom and Gomorrah. Angels are spirits, but we see them here in flesh as human beings. Demons are here to torment in any shape or form. But we have been given authority to cast them out in Jesus' name. Praise the Lord!

FROM A PLAYBOY TO A PROPHET

Ever since I was a little boy, I was tormented by fear—fear of the dark, fear of the unknown, and fear of rejection. I have two brothers and two sisters and I am in the middle. As a teenager, I was struck by an illness. I had been to many hospitals and had seen many doctors. None of them could find out what was wrong with me.

On top of this I contracted tuberculosis. At the time there was no cure for it. I started vomiting blood from my mouth and my nose. I was bone-thin, until Jesus healed me in 1972.

In 1990, the enemy started attacking my family and business. However, that tragedy brought me back to Christ, and because of it my children and I are very close to each other. They love the Lord and are born again. My daughter is in fashion design college. She plans to start were I left off.

I always say, "I do not like the devil, and the devil does not like me." He was after my life and my family for many years. Now I am after him. Wherever I find him, I cast him out in Jesus' name.

After I left the Apostolic International Bible College, I was led astray from the Lord for many years (until I rededicated my life to Him in 1990). My main weakness was for "Jezebel." Women, money, drugs, and expensive, luxurious cars became part of my life. Yet, I had no peace. I just felt empty.

I was a very successful businessman. I was a major manufacturer and retailer of swimwear, sportswear, and lingerie in southern California and all around the United States. I was also a distributor of trashy lingerie to many strip clubs. I traveled and lived in different parts of the world. I thought I was happy, but I always felt empty.

The day came that I had to make a decision between life and death. By God's grace, I chose life. I have since rededicated my life to Him and I try to live right and holy. Now I have a joy unspeakable. I have the joy of the Holy Spirit. I am living clean, pure, and holy. I am possessed by God.

Weeks after I made that decision, the Lord started to work in my life with good measure. I began to see visions and dreams. The God of many chances has been so good and merciful to me. I am now a distributor of the good news, the gospel of the Lord Jesus Christ, my friend, the Man from Galilee. I am not after women any longer. I am after souls, souls, souls, souls—for the heart of the Lord is souls. Glory to His name!

You see, if God could change me, He can change you. If He could use me, He can use you. Only God could turn a playboy into a prophet. God is not a respecter of persons (Acts 10:34, KJV). I am now operating under a prophetic, apostolic, and healing anointing gift. Just turn yourself in. Let the master Craftsman work on your life!

> Come to Me, all you who labor and are heavy laden, and I will give you rest. Take My yoke upon you and learn from Me, for I am gentle and lowly in heart, and you will find rest for your souls. For My yoke is easy and My burden is light.
>
> —Matthew 11:28–30

9

SPECIAL ANOINTING FOR MINISTRY

IT WAS ON a Monday when the three-day intense spiritual cleansing started. The first day I felt a great power emerging from inside me. I was standing and my body started shaking. I saw smoke coming out of my eyes, my ears, and my head. There was smoke coming out from all over my body, like steam in a car wash. I could see the dirt coming out of my body. It smelled like industrial toxins. That was some kind of cleansing.

On Tuesday, the power of the Holy Spirit stormed the place I was in. I saw a physical wind; I could see it and feel it. It entered my body, which started shaking and groaning. God's mighty power was cleansing, purifying, and preparing me for His ministry.

The third day of cleansing was different from the other two. The Spirit of the Lord led me to a place where there were several sprinkler-like showers on a pond. I had a towel on me when I got there. The Spirit would lead me and stop me in each of the sprinklers to be cleansed by the shower of very fine rain. There were seven sprinklers in that place. After the seventh shower, I noticed I was suddenly wearing a white T-shirt. It was one of many preparations for my ministry.

FLYING LIKE AN EAGLE

Flying in an airplane is something, but flying like a bird is another thing. I have experienced it many times in the Spirit. In each of the visitations, I would feel the presence of the Lord with groaning. Then I would be lifted up or caught up in the Spirit and begin flying like a bird. Sometimes the Spirit of the Lord would take me far into the heavenlies and then bring me back to Earth. Sometimes for a short trip I would just find myself flying over specific places or cities. These were tremendous experiences. They brought a whole new meaning to the term *joyride*. When I was flying my arms were stretched out like a bird's wings, with nothing carrying me but the Holy Spirit.

THE IMPARTATION OF THE TWO ANGELS

Once when I was coming out from a Sunday church service, I was met by an angel. As we were having a conversation, a mighty force of power came out from him and entered my body. The power sucked me into him. This happened a few times. As this impartation was taking place, I saw another angel join him. This time the power was so intense I was pulled back and forth, sucked in and out of the angel's power until I was full of that anointing. The Lord Jesus sent me His angels to impart the power I needed for ministry. The Lord Himself also spent time imparting His power to me, as I mentioned earlier in this book.

10

THE TRIBULATION

ONCE, IN A vision, I was in an "underground" church—a secret place of worship—with other persecuted Christians. I heard a loud noise in the air, and when I looked up I saw many airplanes in the sky. The pilots of the planes were shooting people on the ground. I saw many people running and being destroyed. This was during the evening hours and the sky was filled with lightning. People were trying to hide wherever they could, behind rocks and under bushes. But the rocks and the bushes could not shield them from the wrath of the planes, which represented the wrath of God. Let us read from Revelation 6:15–16:

> And the kings of the earth, the great men, the rich men, the commanders, the mighty men, every slave and every free man, hid themselves in the caves and in the rocks of the mountains and said to the mountains and the rocks, "Fall on us and hide us from the face of Him who sits on the throne and from the wrath of the lamb!"

THE BEAST AND I

Right after the Lord showed me the warplanes, He took me to another place, where I saw many people gathered in the streets outside a huge temple. As I was standing with the people and gazing at the tower on top of the temple, I saw a tall man dressed in a business suit appear there. The people were standing still, as if they were waiting for him to say something. This was a temple built by the Antichrist.

The man looked down from the tower and identified himself as the messiah. As I was troubled with what I had just heard, the Lord showed me another vision. In that vision, I saw a large TV screen in the middle of the street. When I came closer to see what was on it, I saw the image of a man from the chest up to the top of his head. He must have been in his late forties. I came closer to the screen and asked him, "What is your name and who are you?" He answered, "My name is Brimstone and I am the Messiah." He was the Beast I had just seen in the previous vision. The Bible says:

> The devil, who deceived them, was cast into the lake of fire and brimstone where the beast and the false prophet are. And they will be tormented day and night forever and ever.
>
> —Revelation 20:10

City Under Siege

> Then I saw another beast coming up out of the earth, and he had two horns like a lamb and spoke like a dragon. And he exercises all the authority of the first beast in his presence, and causes the earth and those who dwell in it to worship the first beast, whose deadly wound was healed. He performs great signs, so that he even makes fire come down from heaven on the earth in the sight of men. And he deceives those who dwell on the earth by those signs which he was granted to do in the sight of the beast, telling those who dwell on the earth to make an image to the beast who was wounded by the sword and lived. He was granted power to give breath to the image of the beast, that the image of the beast should both speak and cause as many as would not worship the image of the beast to be killed. He causes all, both small

and great, rich and poor, free and slave, to receive a mark on their right hand or on their foreheads.

—Revelation 13:11–16

In this vision the hand of the Lord came upon me and caught me up in the Spirit and sat me down in the midst of a troubled city. This city was under the control of the beast and his false prophet. Gunshot was everywhere and I saw many soldiers armed with machine guns patrolling the city. I saw bodies that had been shot strewn through the streets. Then I saw in the distance what looked like a check point. When I came closer to it I saw that many people were being checked to verify if they had the mark of the Beast on them. Even with all the soldiers around, I was able to go through them undetected. I was covered by the blood of Jesus.

CLOSE ENCOUNTERS WITH THE FALSE PROPHETS

In this vision I saw people conducting business in a bustling open-air marketplace. They were buying and selling goods of all kinds. As I was walking and observing the streets of that city, I saw that the false prophets were also busy spreading their false teaching. I saw a woman by the street corner. She had a book in her hands and she was speaking to the people in the street. She was one of the false prophets. In every city I entered I encountered the false prophets. After I left one city, I found myself in a residential area. I saw three false prophets in "sheep's clothing" (Matt. 7:15) moving in and out of the houses.

I determined that I would go after the people and the false prophets. I began telling the people that there is only one Messiah, Jesus Christ, the Son of the living God. I tell you the truth, the people did not seem to care about the true gospel. But their lack of interest did not stop me from preaching to them.

Beware of false prophets, who come to you in sheep's clothing, but inwardly they are ravenous wolves.

—Matthew 7:15

I Was Captured by the Antichrist

In this vision, I found myself in solitary confinement. I was in a high-security area behind a fifty-foot iron fence. My cell was guarded by four soldiers armed with machine guns. I was sitting in a chair with two soldiers standing on my left and the other two on my right.

A very tall man wearing a business suit entered my cell. I knew him immediately. He was the man at the temple in a previous vision who declared he was the messiah. The spirit in him knew the Spirit in me. He entered the cell with the intention of working on my soul to possess me for himself. I heard the Beast talking. Then I saw him coming closer. He knelt down and put his forehead against my forehead. He started meditating, imparting his spirit into my soul.

I closed my eyes and suddenly I saw the Lord Jesus Christ on the cross. He was looking into my eyes. Power was coming out of His piercing eyes and flowing into mine. My body started shaking under the anointing. Even the Beast had to pull himself away from me. The Antichrist became upset, mad, and disappointed. The power in me had resisted the power in him. I saw him leaving the cell angry and discouraged. The power of the devil is limited. God's power is unlimited. For "greater is he that is in [us] than he that is in the world" (1 John 4:4).

Beheaded for Christ

And I saw thrones, and they sat on them, and judgment was committed to them. Then I saw the souls of those who had been beheaded for they are witness to Jesus and for the word of God, who had not worshiped the beast or his image, and had not deceived his mark on their foreheads or on their hands. And they lived and reigned with Christ for a thousand years. But the rest of the dead did not live again until the thousand years were finished. This is the first resurrection. Blessed and holy is who he has part in the first resurrection. Over such the second death has no power, but they shall be priests of God and of Christ, and shall reign with Him a thousand years.

—Revelation 20:4–6

Then the second angel poured out his bowl on the sea, and it became blood as of a dead man; and every living creature in the sea died. Then the third angel poured out his bowl on the rivers and springs of water, and they became blood. And I heard the angel of the waters saying, "You are righteous, O Lord, The One who is and who was and who is to be, Because You have judged these things. For they have shed the blood of saints and prophets, And You have given them blood to drink. For it is their just due."

—Revelation 16:3–6

Once in a dream that I had, I was led by the Spirit of the Lord into the middle of a large park full of many people. In this park I noticed wooden stocks where the faithful Christians had been beheaded because they refused to carry the mark of the Beast. As I was walking through the park I saw a water fountain, from which people were drinking.

Suddenly I saw the water turn into blood, but the people continued drinking. They became intoxicated. I was so disturbed by what I was seeing that I shouted, "Don't drink from it. It is innocent people's blood!" But the people would not listen to me and continued drinking the blood. I continued to walk through the park.

11

VISIONS AND DREAMS

FTER I SAW the bloody drinking water, I had another dream. In this dream I saw people on the street, cars on the road, and people in the park. All of these people stopped and gazed at the sky as if something were going on. When I looked up to the clear, blue sky I saw thick, white clouds forming. The clouds became one and grew larger and larger. A figure emerged out of the white cloud. From the waist up he was wearing a white suit. It was evangelist Benny Hinn. He was looking down at the people gazing at the sky. He started speaking to them, but the people were standing still, frozen like statues, gazing at the sky.

I noticed that the evangelist noticed me looking at him. I started communicating with him, and when I turned around to see the people they were still frozen. No cars were moving. The people looked like the dead. The place looked like a ghost city. When I looked back to the sky, I saw the evangelist merge back into the cloud.

I immediately had another dream. In this one I was taken in the Spirit to India. I saw myself and Benny Hinn riding a double-seated bike that had two sets of pedals. He was sitting in the front and I was sitting in the back. We were pedaling down the street at a high speed when I saw a small, narrow tunnel. I was thinking, "How will we fit through that narrow tunnel?" But we squeezed through it, came out the other side of the tunnel, and parked the bike.

Pastor Benny went into the house next to where we parked the bike. A few minutes later I looked through the window to see the inside room engulfed in flames. I saw a man burning. His flesh was melting and his body turned into a skeleton and fell apart. I saw another man run out from that room with his clothes on fire. The man was about seven feet tall. He tried to fight the fire, but the fire consumed him. I saw him burn until he was just a skeleton turning to ashes. As I was watching this, the Spirit of the Lord spoke to my heart: those were the two stronghold demons that held India for many years. I then came out of the dream.

I have been a covenant partner with Benny Hinn's ministry for many years. I consider him a man of integrity, a prophet of God to the nations of the world, and one of God's generals. He is my spiritual father and mentor, as Katherine Kuhlman was to him.

CITY UNDER WATER

In a dream the Lord showed me a city under water. I was touring around the streets, alleys, and houses that were under water. I saw dead bodies floating everywhere. During my dream I did not know the name of the devastated city.

After this dream, I had another dream of a city under water. I saw evangelist Jesse Duplantis on his bike crossing the flood to a safe place.

Every time the Lord shows me a dream or a vision I write it in my journal. Both of these dreams became reality a few months after the Lord showed them to me. The disaster scenes I saw were caused by Hurricane Katrina in 2005.

TOWERING INFERNO (L.A.)

A month after the hurricane flooded New Orleans, I was reading through my journal and came across these two entries. In April 2005 I had a vision of a ball of fire hitting downtown Los Angeles. This happened a few minutes after I left downtown L.A. and was heading to Venice Beach on the I-10 freeway. I heard what sounded like a bomb explosion. When I looked out my rear window, I saw a large ball of fire fall from the sky and strike the high-rises downtown.

A few minutes later I heard and saw another ball of fire strike Venice Beach. As I was driving, the traffic stopped and I could not go any farther. Cars were parked right in front of me, but they were all empty. I got out of my car and then noticed a sign by the bridge where I was standing. It read "Christ refuge." I followed the direction of the sign, which led me down under the bridge. There I saw many people wearing white gowns. They were all safely protected from the attack.

A few months before this vision of Los Angeles and Venice, California, I had a similar vision of a ball of fire falling from the sky and striking near the Van Nuys Airport. The ball of fire was so strong it split the earth in half. I saw children running from it and I helped them to the safety of a nearby church.

WEST AFRICA

I saw the continent of Africa in the sky. The continent looked like brown clay. It was as large as a football field. Then I saw a ball of fire emerging from the very corner of West Africa. I saw the ball of fire and people thrown to Earth.

ETHIOPIA

I saw a great flood coming from the hills of Ethiopia. The flood covered the capital city of the northern part of Ethiopia, called Makalle. Then I saw two great streams come out and join with the mighty flood.

A year after this dream, I had another dream about a flood in this same city. I was standing by a dry river. Suddenly I saw a little stream of pure water emerging from that dry river. The stream swelled into a large river that covered the city. I then saw a cloud of the Holy Spirit cover the area where I was standing. The cloud moved and hovered above the city.

12

THROWN INTO PRISON

IN 1974 THERE was a great revival in Ethiopia, which was then followed by a period of great persecution. The church of Christ was persecuted and challenged as the largest Pentecostal church (Full Gospel Believers' Church) came under attack.

As a result of the revival, the Pentecostal church was quickly growing. It went from having about three hundred members to over one thousand in just one year. The hand of the Lord was upon the church, as was seen by various signs and wonders. I saw people healed and demons cast out.

In February 1974 the church of Christ came under attack from hypocritical, opposing clergy and slanderous, relentless city officials. They were led by the Coptic Orthodox Church and the late emperor Haile Selassie of Ethiopia, who proclaimed himself to be the King of kings and the Lion of Judah. The Orthodox Church and the emperor issued a warrant for the arrest of all Pentecostal believers and closed all the Pentecostal churches in the country.

One Sunday morning an army stormed the Full Gospel Believers' Church while a service was in progress. We were led at gunpoint to the army's vehicles and then brought to the various police stations across the city. After spending two weeks in police custody, during which time we were bitten and tortured, we were sent to the state prison for six months. We were accused of being in violation of the law for holding an unauthorized meeting.

The only recognized church in the eyes of the "Pharisees" was the Orthodox church, which was the state-approved church. The state and the Orthodox church worked hand in hand for centuries.

And it was the state church that kept the Emperor Selassie in power for over fifty years.

On that particular Sunday morning, there were over a thousand men, women, and children in attendance at the Pentecostal service. After the brutal invasion we were all scattered to different police stations in the capital city, Addis Ababa, which had a population of two million at the time. The officers beat us with their batons. I was held in a ten-foot by ten-foot jail cell, along with a hundred others. Most of us sat on the dusty floor in the fetal position because there was not enough room to stretch our legs. We were held in police custody for two weeks, which was unconstitutional because we had yet to see a judge. We were tortured, bitten, spit upon, and forbidden to go outside for fresh air. We had to urinate in a large container inside the cell.

After two weeks in the police jail, we were brought to court for the hearing. News media from all over the world came to cover the persecution of Christians in that horn of Africa. The BBC, *Newsweek*, the *Times*, and reporters from many other stations and magazines were on the scene. When we appeared before the judge, we were not allowed to say anything but "guilty" or "not guilty." Many Christians were sent to state prison for six months. Every woman that went to prison was forced to shave her head upon arrival. Because of the torture and poor conditions in the prison, we lost two brothers and many fell sick and were left to die. After I was released, I left for Europe to further my study at the Apostolic International Bible College in Denmark.

A month later, in July 1974, the emperor and his fellow ministers were killed by the new military junta who took control of Ethiopia. From 1974 to 1994 the church of Christ went underground. After enduring many years of persecution, the church body is now growing. There are more than two hundred spirit-filled churches in Addis Ababa alone, and that number is still growing. Today, Ethiopia has a democratic government and the freedom of worship.

13

TESTIMONIES

Lieutenant Bill, Vietnam veteran: fifteen years with stomach cancer, left to die

I REMEMBER ONE TBN caller, a Vietnam veteran named Lieutenant Bill. In all my years of ministry I have never heard a man cry like a baby because of the excruciating pain he was experiencing. He had endured cancer of the stomach for fifteen years. Doctors gave up on him. As I was listening to him, I felt compassion for this man. I began to ask the Lord to heal him. I knew in my spirit he was going to be healed. Under a mighty anointing, I told Lieutenant Bill to place his hand on his stomach as a point of contact. As I commanded the devil of cancer to come out of him, I felt a power flowing through me. The pain left him. I heard him saying, "I am healed. The pain is gone. I am healed! I am healed! I felt heat moving in my stomach. The pain is gone." A week later Lieutenant Bill called Trinity Broadcasting Network's prayer department and gave his testimony that he was completely healed from stomach cancer. His testimony is in my file at TBN.

Demonic cancer: "Cancer ate my lungs."

A man with terminal cancer asked me for prayer. I could not hear a word that he was speaking because his throat, his lungs, and chest were eaten by the cancer. His vocal chords were gone. All I could hear was him whispering, "Cancer, cancer." The Spirit of the Lord spoke to my heart to cast the demons of cancer out of him. I did. The demons started to manifest and came out one by one by the man coughing. When the last demon left him he could breathe well. His voice came back, and the tightness in his chest and all the pains were gone. He was completely delivered.

Let me make something clear: not all cancers are demonic, even though the devil is behind all sickness. God is a good God.

Robin: "I felt power all over me."

Robin had head, back, and heart pain for many years. When I prayed for her I felt the anointing of God going through my body. I asked Robin, "What are you feeling in your body?" She answered, "A power of God." I instructed Robin to check if all the pain had gone. She said, "Yes! Yes! Yes!"

Matthew: "I am hearing voices."

Matthew was suffering from bipolar disorder. He heard voices on a regular basis. In fact, they had been troubling him since he was young boy. I asked Matthew if there was anyone in his family's history with bipolar disorder. He mentioned a few. I knew I was dealing with strongholds and generational curses. I commanded the spirit to leave him and for family curses to be broken. A few months later he called and testified that all the troubling voices were gone. He was completely delivered.

Let me make a remark about mental illness: from my experience and the Word of God, I believe most of the time it is demonic. Matthew was troubled by the enemy's voices. The Word of God says, "My sheep hear my voice, and I know them, and they follow me" (John 10:27).

Maria: "My car stalled."

Sister Maria was driving her car on the freeway one night around ten o'clock Eastern time. Suddenly her car stalled and would not start. She called TBN's prayer hotline. The first thing I told her was not to panic. Then I heard that small voice saying, "Remember the fig tree that Jesus cursed and the storm Jesus spoke to?" I said, "Yes, Lord." The voice said, "Then do what Jesus did!"

This was my prayer: "Jesus spoke to the tree, and the tree heard Him. He spoke to the wind, and the wind responded to Him. Now, car, hear the word of the Lord. In the name of Jesus, start!" I instructed the lady to turn the key in the ignition. The car started. I could hear her rejoicing.

Every creation of God has an ear to hear. Jesus said, "If they [the people] keep quiet [and do not praise Him], the stones will cry out" (Luke 19:40, niv). Even the stones have ears to hear the voice of the Lord. After all, the world was created by the spoken word.

"My refrigerator stopped working."

There was an elderly lady on Social Security who was a regular caller. In the past, I had prayed for her for several things. This time she was a little sad. Her refrigerator had given up on her, and she did not have enough money to buy a new one. She wanted me to pray for her finances.

Here again, that small voice of the Holy Spirit spoke to my heart: "Tell her to lay her hands on the broken refrigerator." I did. I then prayed the same prayer I prayed for the car. I said, "Jesus spoke to the fig tree, and the fig tree heard Him. He spoke to the storm, and the storm obeyed Him. Now! Refrigerator, I command you in the name of Jesus, start!" It did. Every time she called TBN she would say, "Asfaw, the refrigerator is still working."

"I am on an Oxygen tank."

"I am on oxygen support, but I believe the Lord can heal me." I knew this woman had faith because I received the confirmation of the Holy Spirit. I told her, "The Lord is going to heal you right now." I prayed a simple prayer: "Holy Spirit, breathe upon this woman's lung, for Jesus Christ's sake." The Holy Spirit spoke to me, "Tell her to breathe in and out three times." The woman did, and the Lord healed her. A week later the same woman called Trinity Broadcasting Network to report that she was healed completely—no more oxygen support. I could tell you hundreds upon hundreds of testimonials like this.

"Cancer ate my body."

"I have cancer all over my body and in my bones. I am in a wheelchair. I am a churchgoing woman, but I haven't been to church in a long time." As she was telling me her story, I was listening to the Holy Spirit, as I always do when I am praying for people. I commanded the demon of cancer to bow to the Name above every other name. The power of God went through her body. I told her to get up from her wheelchair and walk, in Jesus' name. She did and she walked. She said, "I can't wait until I go to my church this coming Sunday. My pastor and the church will be surprised." She was so happy. Our God is a good God.

Shawn: "Doctors gave up on me."

Shawn had pain in her head, back, and all over her body. When I heard her voice on the phone, I felt a very sharp pain course through my body. I knew by the word of knowledge that I was experiencing or feeling what she felt. I commanded the pain to leave her body. It did. The pain in her head and her back were all gone. She started shouting, "Yes! Yes! Thank you, Lord!"

She was surprised how I knew that she had pain in her brain. I told her, "By the word of knowledge. When I am operating in the word of knowledge, I will feel pain in the same organ or area that the person I'm praying for is feeling. Or I can hear that small voice telling me by name. For example, I will hear 'kidney' or 'heart' or any part of an organ." When the Lord gives me the word of knowledge, the person I'm praying for gets healed.

Tina: "Tumor in my brain"

Tina had a problem similar to Shawn's; she had a very sharp pain in her brain. She told me she had had it for many years. Tina had a tumor in her brain. The same word of knowledge came upon me and I felt a very sharp pain in my brain. It felt as if someone put a knife right in the center of my head. Tina did not get a chance to tell me what I should pray for. The very second I heard her voice on the phone and felt the pain I commanded that tumor to disappear in Jesus' name. The pain was gone and Tina believed she was healed from the brain tumor.

Jerome: "My toe is killing me."

Jerome had diabetes, which was affecting his leg and toe. The word of knowledge came upon me and I felt sharp pain in my left toe. Jerome had pain from diabetes in his left toe. God healed him.

The gift of knowledge reveals to me before the person tells me anything about their problem. I either hear the voice of God or I begin feeling the same way that person is feeling. Sometimes I will ask the person why the Lord is showing me something. I'll say, "Does this thing mean anything to you?" The person then confirms the word I received.

"I am not pregnant, I have a tumor."

I remember a few years ago, when the Lord first gave me the gifts of the Spirit, a woman asked me to pray for a tumor she was carrying in her stomach. She said, "I look like I'm nine-months pregnant. But I am not pregnant. I have a very large tumor in my stomach." As I was listening to her, the Lord spoke to me to tell her put her hands on her stomach as a point of contact. She did. I only spoke a few words: "Tumor, melt in Jesus' name." Right after I commanded the tumor to melt, the woman said her stomach went flat immediately. The tumor disappeared. Brothers and sisters, just speak the Word. The Word works only if you work it.

Henry

Henry had been suffering from the effects of a stroke for a long time. The word of knowledge came to me and I called out the stroke and prayed for him. He can now move his arms, legs, and neck. He received an instant healing.

Jamara

Jamara had been suffering from kidney failure. Pain would constantly shoot all over her body. By the word of knowledge I told her, "The Lord is going to heal you." After I rebuked the sickness, the pain left her. She believed the Lord also healed her kidney.

Ruth

Ruth asked me to pray for a man who had cancer. He was not expected to live. While I was praying for the man, the Holy Spirit brought to my attention to pray for Ruth. She had a foot problem. When I told her what the Lord just told me, she was surprised. She said, "How did you know? Did the Lord tell you?" I said, "Yes." The Lord healed her right away. These are just a few of hundreds of testimonies to lift up your spirit. Jesus is still the Healer. Just believe!

Edith: Parkinson's disease and shaking syndromes

Edith said, "My body is shaking violently. I have Parkinson's disease. I am in pain. Please pray for me." As I was led by the Holy Spirit, I said to Edith, "Do you believe that the Lord can heal you right now?" She said, "Yes."

I began praying and took authority over the disease. I knew in the spirit she had been touched by God almighty. I asked Edith if the shaking was gone. She said all the pain and all the shaking were gone. She said, "I can move my fingers and my arms, which I could not do before." Praise the Lord forevermore.

Fred: "My wife is back home."

"This afternoon you prayed for me, for my wife to come home. She left me and my children months ago. A few hours after your prayer, she called me from the airport. She is coming home." This was the day before Valentine's Day. That is what I love about my Jesus. He is the God of love and restoration. I was so happy for them.

Adala and daughter: Pituitary gland

A mother asked for prayer for her daughter. Before she told me what the problem was, I knew by the word of knowledge and called out brain sickness. The woman answered, "My daughter, Lisa, has a problem with her pituitary gland." I did not even know what the pituitary gland was until she explained it to me. I prayed and commanded her daughter to be healed in Jesus' name. When I am operating with the word of knowledge the person always receives healing.

Debra: Degenerative disc

As I prayed for Debra, I felt strong anointing on me. I said to her, "What is going on with your body?" She said, "The power of God is flowing. My pain is gone, and I can move my arms and my back. I am healed! Thank God!"

Delma: Tumor in a child's chest

A mother asked me to pray for her eleven-year-old son. She said, "My son has a tumor in the left side of his chest. Please pray for him." In an authoritative voice I said, "Where is your son?" She said, "He is sitting here." I said, "Lay your hand on his chest." As I was commanded the tumor to be gone I heard the child shouting, "It disappeared! It is gone!"

Brothers and sisters, I hope these testimonies give you hope, for Christ is the hope of glory (Col. 1:27).

Arty

A few years ago a tree fell on Arty injuring his shoulder and dislocating his arm. A word of knowledge came to me and I felt a pain in my shoulder. I was feeling what he was feeling. After

I prayed for him, I instructed him to do what he could not do before. He said, "There is no pain. I can move my arm, which I could not do before." He was healed completely.

Judy: "I am blind in both my eyes."

Judy had only 3 percent of her eyesight. This was my prayer: "Lord, eyes are meant to see. Now, you blind spirit, come out of her! Open! Lord, let your light shine on her and disperse the darkness. I thank you, Lord, for hearing me; you always hear me." Right after I prayed, I instructed Judy to read something. She said, "I am feeling heat on my eyes. My eyes are getting clearer." She started reading a book. The Lord, in His mercy healed her.

✳ ✳ ✳ ✳

I hope you are blessed and encouraged by these testimonies.

> The works that I do shall he do also; and greater works than these shall he do.
>
> —John 14:12

Just believe.

A SINNER'S PRAYER

I F YOU HAVE never received Christ as your personal Savior, you can pray this prayer with me:

> *Father, I know that I am a sinner. And I ask you to forgive me. I believe Christ died for me and I want to turn from my sins. Jesus, come into my heart and be my personal Lord and Savior. I promise to obey You and follow You all the days of my life. Amen.*

If you have prayed this prayer with me and believed what you prayed, you are now saved. Remember, there is no sin from the pit of hell that the blood of Jesus cannot wash.

If you are a fallen minister, get up and get back in the Word. The Scripture tells us in Proverbs 24:16, "For a righteous man may fall seven times And rise again, But the wicked shall fall by calamity."

LETTERS FROM READERS

In your book *Heaven Is Empty, Hell Is Full* you mentioned that the Lord showed you a city in the northern part of Ethiopia called Mekelle under a great flood. Three days ago, the fourth of May 2008, that city the Lord showed you was under disastrous flood with many casualties; the land that we know is not the same. It was shown on the Ethiopia Television Network. Surely the vision that the Lord has shown you has come to pass.

—Brother Seged
Addis Ababa, Ethiopia

I have received a copy of your book *Heaven Is Empty, Hell Is Full*. It was indeed a most stirring and faith-building book. I really enjoyed and appreciated reading your life story and revelations of heaven and hell. Many thanks for writing this book. I hope it will be well received among born-again Christians worldwide and that it will be a great testimony to those not yet saved. God bless you all until He comes!

—Carl-Gustav Forslund, Sweden

I read your book *Heaven Is Empty, Hell Is Full*, which was given to me by Sister Choo Thomas, who is very close friend of mine. It is powerful, awakening messages of Jesus' heart in the last days. Jesus is grieving over His bodies (churches) that are in deep sleep. God is raising many hidden servants like you to shake the churches. I pray that the anointing of the Holy Spirit would spread out and touch many souls through your ministry.

—Pastor Michael, Orange county, California

I just finished reading your book a few days ago; it was awesome! I do feel like it transformed my life. I am very grateful for your sharing your experiences in your book. It was such a blessing.

If I may, I'd like to tell you a little about myself. I went to a Baptist church when I was a teenager for about six years and then they closed the doors for good because they couldn't keep a preacher there. I tried to get in another church for the last twenty years and couldn't do it. I started living the way I wanted, for the world and in sin. Four years ago I started reading the Bible and spiritual books and came across Choo Thomas's Web site. I saw her thirty-eight-minute video, and something changed in me. I went to a local Barnes and Noble bookstore and bought a copy of *Heaven Is So Real*; it was the only copy they had at the time. I wanted the book so bad, and I have since read it five times. Every time I read it I felt like I learned something new. For the last four years I have been buying copies of the book, burning [copies of] her video and Bill Weise's video *23 Minutes in Hell*, and witnessing with them by giving them out for free. I am not rich or wealthy, I am just trying to be the hands and feet of Jesus and tell people how much He loves us and how soon He is coming back.

I have rededicated my life to Christ and I don't ever want to go back to my old life. I want to serve the Lord with all my heart. I love Him very much! And I have learned to love others. I talked to Sister Choo a month ago and it was so amazing and very humbling for me. She has helped me so much in my walk with the Lord and I am very grateful to her. If you get a chance, would you please write back at your convenience. I would love to hear from you. God bless you.

—Buddy

I just finished reading your book this morning. It probably took me a day and a half to read it. I just wanted to say that I was blessed by it and learned a lot. There is a lady who goes by the name of Choo Thomas. I don't know if you have heard of her, but she saw a lot of the same things that you did. She has a book out called *Heaven Is So Real*. That is a very anointed book as well.

I have always been fascinated by books on heaven and revelation. I pray that the Lord may use me as well for His glory and His purpose. I pray for the indwelling of the Holy Spirit. There are a lot of churches that will not give themselves over to the Holy Spirit and let Him do a miracle work in their services. It is such a blessing that you give the Holy Spirit the complete freedom to do whatever He wants. That is why you are so blessed! Well, keep up the good work, my friend, and I pray that you and your family are prospering, even as your souls prosper.

—Unsigned letter

One day I was very depressed and I picked up your book *Heaven Is Empty, Hell Is Full*. As I started reading it, I felt something jump up from my body, and all the depression was gone. I felt the anointing of God was in that book. Thank you for your obedience to the Lord in writing this book.

—Gary, Anaheim, California

I have started reading the book and I couldn't stop until I finished it. You have opened my mind about what hell and heaven look like. Thank you, Brother.

—Debbie, Pomona, California

Brother Asfaw's book on heaven and hell will give you chills. One about the excitement of heaven and the presence of God; the other about hell, the sight of people in the flames screaming. Jesus told Evangelist Asfaw to tell the world and all Christians alike, "Fill up heaven, not hell!"

—Pastors J. and W., El Monte, California

I have read and finished the book *Heaven Is Empty, Hell Is Full*. I was so blessed and inspired by it. Especially the testimonies of people who had been miraculously healed when you prayed for them. I believe these testimonies will encourage and build up the faith of believers and non-believers. Thank you.

—J., San Fernando Valley, California

I read your book *Heaven Is Empty, Hell Is Full*, and I believe everything you said in the book because I myself have experienced and seen the living Christ a few years ago. Be encouraged; the Lord is opening more doors for you. No devil in hell can stop it! Thank you, Brother.

—S., Orange County, California

I heard about your book and I ordered a copy of it. Right after I got it, I started reading and couldn't stop until I finished. I was so impressed about how the Lord showed you His generals and the two prophetesses falling into an error. It is about time the Lord is cleaning His house. Thank you, Brother, for being used by the Lord.

—C., Texas

I just finished the book now. This is an awesome testimony about one who encountered Jesus and visited heaven and hell. Whoever has doubted about heaven, please read this book. Heaven is so real; also, hell is real.

I want no one to go to hell. This book will help you to know how heaven is and how we can go to heaven. Jesus is only way to go heaven. Wait for the Rapture with a pure heart and holy life.

—Jun

NOTES

Chapter 7

THE WORD WORKS IF YOU WORK IT

1. Peter J. Madden, *The Wigglesworth Standard* (New Kensington, PA: Whitaker House, 2000).

TO CONTACT THE AUTHOR

Solomon's Temple International Healing Ministry
P.O. Box 2402
Van Nuys, CA 91404

E-mail: SolomonTempleMin@aol.com

Web site: www.heavenisempty.com

RECOMMENDED READING